LIFE IS JUST
A BOWL OF
CHOICES

LIFE IS JUST A BOWL OF CHOICES

Robyn Russell

Library of Congress Control Number:		2018902781
ISBN:	Hardcover	978-1-5434-8919-4
	Softcover	978-1-5434-8918-7
	eBook	978-1-5434-8917-0

Print information available on the last page.

Rev. date: 03/23/2018

To order additional copies of this book, contact:
Xlibris
800-056-3182
www.Xlibrispublishing.co.uk
Orders@Xlibrispublishing.co.uk
773761

CONTENTS

LIFE IS JUST A BOWL
OF CHOICES

The choices we live by, whether our own or those made on our behalf, decide our future path in life. Throughout this life we are often given the opportunity to change the direction we are taking. Much depends on your own nature and character as to how the choice you make will affect not only you, but those around you.

For many of us we lay the blame for our misfortunes and troubles on those who made those choices rather than looking to ourselves for going along with it all, not looking at the other alternatives or accepting those that we did go along with or had no alternative because we were too young.

For me, I just wish I could be selfish enough to just walk away from some of the choices I have made and not worry about the effect on those around me. My advice to anyone is that you really look into the complexities of each option before taking that step. Involve all those that are likely to be impacted before making a decision and give them a voice. Maybe, just maybe, their arguments are stronger for not taking that route than yours are for doing it.

It pays whenever you are confronted by these conflicting options to create a pros and cons list, and give it a lot of thought before committing yourself. Keep the list for those days when you just wonder why you made that choice/decision. Try to see what the consequences are likely to be, as far as you can, bearing in mind that some choices we make will inevitably lead to unforeseen consequences. Be prepared to change or amend those decisions as the need arises. Nothing is written in stone, well not since the dark ages!

Throughout my book, I hope you will see that some of the choices I have made in my life have been dictated by circumstances, some by other people and some by a sense of love and loyalty. This is who I am now and although I acknowledge the mistakes I have made during my life, my choices, decisions and the resultant consequences, are what have made me this way.

Would I change anything? Do it differently? Make different choices? Probably, but then you cannot change the past and what if's are just that. The most you can do is to live through the highs and lows, be brave enough to change the things you can and learn to live with the one's you can't.

Overall I have made many mistakes through my life which has inadvertently affected so many around me. Some I learnt from, some I have only just realised, and in writing this book I have learnt so much about myself.

INTRODUCTION

Reaching retirement and thinking of the years past that constitutes my life so far, my friends and family convinced me to share my thoughts in the form of a book.

I thought it would be a 'short' story, however, the more I thought about it the more it became a biographical nightmare, full of negativity and self pity.

Wanting to share experiences and yet not bore the reader with my life, I decided to write it more as a series of events, choices, decisions and consequences that made my life what it is today.

The more I shared the more I realised that most if not all people have experienced one or more of these events, that for some reason, the 'powers that be' decided this was to be my life. I blame my Mum for instilling the strength of character in me to stand by the choices and decisions I make and not run away when things get difficult.

I don't pretend to be an expert in any of the events, only to share how they have affected me and how the choices and decisions I made led to the consequences that affected not only me but those around me.

Everything I have written is my story and as my sister says, it doesn't truly reflect the full story, but is a true reflection from my memories and my perspective.

Throughout my life I have met and worked with many brave people who have suffered so much more in their lives, and there is very rarely an easy solution. One thing has become clear to me is that you can choose to allow negative events to affect your life or you can choose to accept them and move on with a more positive outlook. Put things down to experience and learn from your mistakes and try to keep everything in perspective. So many outside influences, from friends, family, associates, colleagues, and social media can often pressure us into having negative thoughts about ourselves, that we find it difficult to deal with life in general.

The wonderful thing about life is that you have it in you to change and make things better not only for yourself but also those around you. Whether this is by walking away from situations or accepting who you are, finding those solutions and accepting help when you need it.

Learning to bite your tongue and pick your arguments rather than ruin a perfectly good relationship by speaking out of turn. Telling someone that they should have done something just makes them feel worse about themselves because they know they should have done it!

It has taken many years for me to realise that there is little point in worrying about something that might happen as often it is that very worry that could drive it to happen. Looking back I see that my distrust in my relationships has been the very thing that has brought my fears into reality.

So my advice is don't go looking for trouble, there will be enough to worry about when it comes. At least then you can actually do something about it.

The sad thing about this is that it takes you a lifetime to learn, when actually you need that knowledge from day one. Relationships would be so much easier, wouldn't they?

Well enough of my gems of genius and back to my story, I hope you find, if nothing else, that you nod along with my experiences, saying to yourself, 'Been there, done that'!

To save the blushes of my off-spring and extended family I have changed their names to protect the innocent and of course save them any embarrassment! The names were chosen by each person so I take no blame for the unusual. Although I must admit that I could cheerfully strangle my husband for his choice of D'Artagnan, well that was until I found the 'Find & Replace' option on the computer!

ME

Writing a book which looks at your own life does lead you naturally to see yourself as others see you. Something we tend not to do or even think about just accepting our character and personality without question.

I do believe that the experiences we have through life are what make us the person we are, and often drastic changes take place that affect both your personality and character.

How we see ourselves is so very different from the way other people see us. So I thought I would write down how I thought about myself, and maybe you as the reader can decide for yourselves what sort of person I am from the experiences I have shared with you.

Overall this is how I see myself:

Hardworking in whatever task/job I undertake
Loving and caring to my family and anyone who needs me.
Good friend that will do anything asked of me (if I can)
Shy, although the years have taught me how to overcome that
Friendly and outgoing with strangers when put in a social or work event
Do not suffer fools gladly although happy to help if they are receptive
Willing to take criticism, although I will fight my corner if I feel the
    criticism is unwarranted
Impossible to live with over the years, although lots of reasons for that
    as you will no doubt see for yourself
Lacking in confidence although I do have a tendency to blow my own
    trumpet especially when not appreciated

Often throughout my life I have heard comments from family, friends and colleagues that I have dismissed without further thought, blaming them for their own issues with me rather than thinking that maybe, just maybe, I am the issue.

I have always thought I was a nice person, willing to help anyone, be there when needed, do my job well, and generally an all round good guy! Some of my friends continue to believe this is who I am, however, this book has made me realise that ultimately I am my own worst enemy. I blame those around me rather than facing the fact that just maybe I am at fault. My moods and innate belief in myself and my abilities causes real issues for those around me.

My nephew recently told me that I was one of the most hard-nosed bitches he had ever met. Although this hurt at the time it did make me realise that I must appear like this to a lot of people as I have tried throughout my life not to allow my emotions to affect the situations I find myself in, whether at work or at leisure.

A close friend also told me the other day that my problem with work and colleagues was that I was too efficient and clever for my own good and therefore people hated working with me as I showed them up. Reading about the jobs I have held and the outcome of most of them makes me realise that they are probably right. Something I have been proud of all my working life has just been blown out of the water!

So a little tip from me to you – just because you were employed to do a job doesn't mean to say they actually want you to be able to do your job well and not make mistakes as this will make everyone around you feel inadequate and lead to despising your competence and abilities. Smiling and being happy doing your job is also a mistake. Getting compliments and excellent feedback from the customers will not save you from the wrath of these incompetents who find it so hard to do the job they are paid to do. However, these are the very people who keep their jobs, get pay rises and are excluded from redundancies. Almost sounds like politics, and we all know how those are the ones that seem to retain their positions and take responsibility for nothing!

So for all my working life I have rubbed up people the wrong way without even realising it. If only I had known at the time, maybe I could have saved myself being used and abused by so called friends and colleagues, not worked so hard, or been so helpful. Maybe, just maybe, life would have been less emotional, easier to deal with and kept my friends if I was more needy.

I do believe in re-incarnation, and just hope that when my soul comes back to claim a new body, I will be a beautiful, needy person, who will spend my whole life relying on someone else.

PROLOGUE

I am a 60+ year old wife of 35 odd years to a dedicated and patient man, D'Artagnan, have 1 son, Ian, and 1 step-daughter, Lisa, who in turn have produced 2 grandchildren, Marie and Anthony. Add to the family my Mother-in-law, Jemima, aged 95 (at the start of writing this book) and a rescue cat, Petie.

I have one brother, Martin, and one sister, Caroline, thankfully where my sister is concerned we have kept in touch and achieved a closeness over the years that we lost after our childhood. It is only since our Mum died that I have established contact once again with Martin.

There are innumerable members of extended families, all of which, for one reason or another, are no longer in my life. I miss them all but have come to accept that this is the nature of families nowadays.

I am an ordinary middle class woman born in 1951 in Mombasa, East Africa, during colonial years as the youngest of 3 children. We lived on the farm of my Father's family. Unfortunately the marriage ended when I was just 3 months old, so my memories of the farm are non-existent.

Mum moved to Eldoret in Kenya and then finally to Tabora in Tanzania before coming home to England in the early 1960s, (I was 10 years old,) where I have remained on the South Coast and built my life.

Both my siblings have travelled extensively, although I have never felt the desire other than a holiday to South Africa, to get married, and a back packing holiday in my 40s to USA, Australia, Fiji and the Cook Islands. There have been visits to Caroline over the years as she moved to Europe. Firstly in Spain and currently Italy where she lives and works and will soon be retiring to Sicily.

Martin, having travelled extensively in his teen years has been settled in England and is a dedicated artist and healer.

I attended a comprehensive school and managed to get some qualifications in Secretarial skills, English and Maths. The rest fell by the wayside as boys and other more interesting things took my attention.

I became a single parent when I was just turned 18, married when my son was 9, taking on D'Artagnan's daughter, Lisa, at the same time, when she was 7.

Both children, now adults, left home and set up their own lives when they were 18 and 17. I have tried hard to be there for both of them when the need arises. Including decorating Lisa's house when she was too pregnant to climb a ladder. Ian has managed to live in a world of his own for most of his life but I have always been there for him whatever his needs. As most parents understand from their own experiences it doesn't actually matter whether you give them a good or bad upbringing, they will still go their own way!

Today I am taking 'happy' pills (anti-depressants) to stop from throwing myself under a train, or off the edge of a very steep cliff. For those of you sceptical of the efficacy of these pills, all I can say is that they work for me! I am not sure who I am anymore as emotionally, for most of the time, I remain in the middle. D'Artagnan, (my husband), who knows me better than anyone, says he doesn't like the way the pills affect me, but agrees that he prefers it in the end having experienced many, many years of highs and lows!

Memories of life in Africa had a rosy glow, being too young to understand the vagaries of human emotion, and the hardship my Mother endured when my father left us when I was 3 months old. How my Mother managed to cope as a single parent with 3 young children shows the strength and determination that I feel she has passed on, at least to the female members of the family.

Caroline told me recently that I have always had a selective memory, remembering bits and pieces rather than whole stories, but I like to think this is down to my 'glass half full' attitude to life, so although the 'glass half empty' is still there, I choose to remember only the positives.

Vague memories of days out, garden parties, running barefoot, learning to ride a bike on a huge farm, days spent watching cattle being 'dipped', chasing lizards down the storm drains to see how many tails we could get, sunshine and carefree days. All in all a childhood to be envied.

Our time in Africa was during the 'colonial' years so life was very different from England although of course at the time I was not aware that there was a difference. Most English families had servants to help with daily life and although we were not too well off we were no different. Mum had always had nannies to look after us, a houseboy and cook to manage the daily running of the house and caring for the animals. We had a house at the bottom of the garden where our workers could live and have their families with them.

To manage 3 children and hold down a full time job is by no means easy, however, Mum got a job as a matron at a boarding school, where she could earn and spend time with us.

After school I remember being cared for by a very pretty woman, can't remember her name, but she had a record player and the very first song I ever tried to emulate was Que Sera by Kathy Kirby. Probably why D'Artagnan now says I have a lovely voice but very Julie Andrews rather than Suzi Quatro! I would have loved to be a singer but perhaps never had the drive to follow it very seriously other than singing in church and pantomimes. Then suddenly I was just too old!

We all three went to a Goan school run by Nuns and Fathers and along with the Commissioners two children, were the only white children at the school. Although to be honest none of us noticed that there was a difference and we had many friends from all the different communities.

Mum made all our clothes while we were in Africa and over the years she made beautiful dresses with smocking. Being an avid knitter, all cardigans and jerseys were made by her. By necessity once we came to England and being the youngest I got all my sister's hand-me-downs. Although to be totally honest, in my teens I would rush home from school and pinch Caroline's clothes and get out the house before she got home! My brother was luckier as trousers were not something Mum could turn her hand to. All our bought clothes came from second hand shops including our school uniforms.

I can't say I was particularly pretty as a child, my sister took that crown, with her long hair and pretty face. Most people would say that I was attractive but prone to puppy fat! I can't say I was particularly a nice child, my sister, once again, took that crown, being nice natured and loving. I knew I was precocious, cheeky and in turns had a nasty side able to hurt both physically and emotionally whenever anyone crossed me. I think all my family would agree with that!

RELATIONSHIPS & FAMILY

For all the interesting things that happened to me when I was young my Mum instilled in us a sense of family, that is as strong in me today as it was then. Of course to have a strong family unit the whole family have to want that too! Events that happen and choices we make can affect not just us but our family members.

As you read on you will see that my relationships have been very hit and miss, some disasters brought about by my own behaviour (more often than not!) and some brought about by others.

Family relationships can change as your life or their life alters or a new dynamic is brought into the mix. This could be an addition to the family, a change in finances or job, or a change to your way of living. Often it is not your reluctance to welcome the change but that of your family members who cannot accept the choices that you have made.

As I have discovered, as much as I want to rectify the rifts which seem to open up like sore wounds, it does take two to tango, make concessions, accept gracefully or agree to disagree, and you can't make others fall in with your thoughts and desires no matter how hard you try.

Both my children, since leaving home, have told me what a bad Mother I was to them, and as I have told them both, I did my best and if that wasn't good enough, then I am sorry. You cannot change what happened during your childhood but you can grow up, put it behind you, and move on with your life. In varying degrees they have both done this, Lisa by cutting me out of her life and living it to the full, and Ian who has decided on a life of dependency, from either me or Social support and cannot get past his perceived awful childhood.

From my point of view, although I worked 6 days a week, Sundays was always spent taking the children out. Summer days it was the beach all day or tramping over the Downs. Going out to special places when we could afford it and visiting family where they had the opportunity to play with their cousins or enjoy their grandparents garden.

The hardest thing for me is trying to hide the hurt and sadness that these events have brought into my life, and believe me, they never go away, no matter how much you outwardly show the world that everything is OK.

MY MUM

Mum was born in Halifax, England to a well to do family, and had 2 brothers and a sister. Unfortunately her youngest brother Brian was killed at Dunkirk during the second world war at the age of 21. She became a nurse at Great Ormond Street, Children's Hospital in London, joined the Army during WW2 where she drove an ambulance and taught women to drive them safely. This was done by placing a glass of water on the bonnet of the ambulance and making them drive over a rough field! She once told me that she couldn't believe her eyes when driving her ambulance in London she encountered a large stuffed giraffe hanging over the telephone wires across the street with a backdrop of planes, bombs and fires. She was schooled in part in Denmark which led to her working for the Danish underground during the final years of the war and received a medal from the Danish King. Stationed in London she would converse over the radio with the many underground spies. Like most people who were involved in the war she kept the more devastating parts of the war to herself. After the war she went out to Africa to see her brother married, met my Father and settled in East Africa.

Never knowing my real dad and wishing I had never met my step dad, my Mum was the one constant in my life. Teaching me everything I needed and like all parents, as I grew older, wondering where she had gone wrong when, as all teenagers, we went our own way, convinced we knew better. Doesn't that just come back and bite you on the bum when you are the Mother with children!

She did a good job, as for all the upsets, trials and tribulations, we never went without and ultimately I had a happy childhood.

Being an avid reader herself every night she would read us stories such as the Just So Stories by Rudyard Kipling and The Kontiki Expedition. She had an amazing way with words turning adult books into exciting adventures. We would bathe and dress in our night clothes and then all three sit on her armchair with one of us designated to brush her hair while she read to us.

Mum didn't cook a lot but when she did we were all in the kitchen with her, 'helping', and of course licking the bowl! There was the inevitable argument as we fought over the spoon and bowl, especially with 3 of us!

She was never heavy 'handed' with us having learned early on in Motherhood that a good sharp smack on the backside or back of the legs hurt her more than us, so it was early on that she resorted to hairbrushes or slippers as the weapons of choice when disciplining us. I never remember her laying either a hand or a brush on me until we came to England, but I think this was due to us having nannies (Ayas) in Africa, who took on that role. Coming to England was a real culture shock for us all, after all none of us children had ever bathed ourselves or been expected to do chores as we had staff to do that. I think with all that Mum took on when moving to England, she really had little idea how to discipline us and therefore resorted to the good sharp smack. No doubt nowadays she would have been arrested for child abuse!

I can remember at the age of 14 sneaking in the back door late one night, creeping up the stairs, changing into my pyjamas and then coming down, convinced that I was doing a good impression of having been in for ages, only to have the dreaded hairbrush. I only did that once and in future kept my clothes on as the smack didn't hurt quite so much. There was of course the inevitable ban on going out after school for a week and my pocket money docked.

Mum always supported me, being there when I needed her and staying in the background when I didn't, not judging me for the mistakes I made but helping me to get through with wise advice and whatever support she was able to give me. She taught me how to drive, about sex (must have missed that bit about the importance of contraception), the difference between right and wrong, and to take responsibility for my actions.

Knowing what I know now about surviving, dealing with relationships and having a family of my own makes me appreciate just how hard a life my Mum must have had. We never see how old they are, or ever see them cry!

I only remember once seeing the despair she felt when we had moved back to England and were living in a flat. There was a flat roof and a bakery next door so waking up to the smell of fresh bread reminds me so much of the times we had there. Our bedroom was in the basement, with no windows, and Mum had painted it bright yellow. It was at this flat that my step father came from Africa and found us. He features quite extensively in my chapter on Domestic Violence and Abuse.

One night Mum sat on the edge of my bed and said that perhaps the best thing was to end it all, but she couldn't leave us alone, so not to worry she would pop something in our night time cocoa and we just wouldn't wake up! Whether this was in my dreams or a reality I never did find out, but I do remember being frightened of going to sleep that night.

I lived with Mum until my son Ian was 3 years old and then when I moved out she went to live with Caroline. Once my sister started working and living abroad Mum decided to join her for a round the world trip they had planned together. I was always amazed at how she just got rid of all her books without a qualm saying that this was the start of a new adventure for her. Each time we moved house, and we moved a lot, we would laugh at her for managing to get rid of maybe 4 books out of her extensive collection. Adding more than the 4 books between moves we would end up with 6 or 7 tea chests of books that would have to be dusted and packed and unpacked each time.

She joined my sister in Spain and unfortunately almost a year later on the eve of buying the car to start their adventures she had a massive stroke and died.

I was fortunate that she had had a minor stroke a month before and I was able to go over and spend a week with her. It was so sad to see that she had lost all the skills that she loved so much, the reading, writing, and knitting. But we laughed and I played (play being the operative word) my saxophone for her. I couldn't bring myself to play again for many years. I still have the letters she wrote to me showing her determination not to be beaten by the stroke.

One day Caroline and I decided to give Mum a shower and as her balance and physical movements had been hit by the stroke we decided to all get in the shower naked together, one of us holding her while the other washed her. It was so hilarious and wasn't helped by the fact that we all got a fit of the giggles at the incongruity of it.

One day sitting there brushing her hair and having a heart to heart she spoke of her life and how she couldn't regret the things that had happened as she felt so lucky to have us 3 children. All in all she felt blessed having had so many adventures and if she was to die now she would die content and happy.

She died at the age of 76 in 1991 and I still cry whenever I think of her and miss her still. I still have a jumper she knitted for me when I was a teenager. Each year I decide to get rid of it but somehow I just can't! During her retirement she took up painting and would go out each week with her art class and have a lovely day out. Her painting was never that good, however, I still have one or two of her artwork on my walls at home. Again I can't bring myself to get rid of them.

I have never been one for taking photographs or keeping momentos and it is only now that I realise what a loss this is. When you can no longer be with them, memories are so important to help you through the grieving process initially and through the rest of your life without them.

You never get over losing your Mum and to this day I still have tears in my eyes whenever I think of her or attempt to speak about her. The feeling of my utter sadness at losing her has been mixed with anger for her leaving me, but also at suddenly being the grown up! I so miss the cuddles, the advice, and her just being there at the end of the phone. Don't waste this precious time as regrets won't bring her back. Spend time with her while you can, if you can't get to see her then set a special time each week to have a good chat or just share your week.

SIBLINGS

I was named after the nurse who walked in when Mum was giving me my first feed and I stopped and turned round to look at her. Of course at my age I couldn't possibly have seen her but it was a trait that was evident throughout my life. Curiosity and not wanting to be left out of anything!

Being the youngest of 3 I suppose I was the most spoilt one and got used to getting my own way at a very young age. It's funny how there would always be 2 of us against the third, and it didn't seem to matter what the combination. To get my own way I would do whatever it takes, cry, scream, tell tales, throw things and generally be a bitch.

I once told Caroline that she was adopted and she believed me. Then there was the time I threw a tin of syrup at her, which, unfortunately, made her very sticky but did not draw blood. However, when I was running away from her wrath I ran straight into the door, cutting my head open. Guess who got the telling off! Caroline, of course!

Once we were dressed as fairies with a wand, and Caroline told me you had to hold the wand to the side, but being me, I insisted it should be held in front. To this day I have the proof that she was right!

My memories of those early years are sparse although I do have some old 8mm film so I know what I looked like at that age! Photographs in albums of when I was born and sitting in my pram with my Ayah show me to be a plump, mischievous child, that butter wouldn't melt in my mouth. I am assured by both Caroline and Martin that I lived up to that description for the rest of my childhood.

Funnily enough we all met up last year as retirees and fell straight back in to being as we were as children with Martin ruling the roost, Caroline quiet and me arguing the toss at every opportunity!

Throughout our childhood Mum encouraged us to understand nature and would keep us off school if any of our animals were having babies. I don't suppose the schools of today would put up with that and no doubt Mum would be fined! How schooling has changed through the years. I can remember lessons where we were taught to write properly, using coloured inks and lined paper. Knowing your tables by heart was just as important as reading. Discipline was something you got when you deserved it. I must admit to having my mouth washed out several times, the cane on my hand more than once and detentions by the dozen.

Caroline was always the prettiest with a nice nature, for all my taking advantage of being the baby of the family, I was always envious of her.

Without her and Mum's support during the first nine years of my son's life I don't think I could have coped. Our relationship has grown so much closer in the last 20 years and I love her dearly. I don't think she has ever forgiven me for pinching her clothes as a teenager, and I don't blame her a bit! I try to make up for all my nastiness now by being there for her and her two children who remained in England when she left home to work abroad. I can't wait for her yearly visit when she manages to get away.

Rhoda (my Ayah) was our mainstay, her mother first looked after Martin and then Rhoda took over when Caroline was born. She was the most lovely lady with her own family and lived in the house at the bottom of the garden. We often found ourselves sitting on the floor of her house eating posha (a type of dumpling) and mutton stew and to this day I can still remember the taste. The wonderful thing about a Nanny, I think, is that the only time we really spent with Mum was when she had the time and inclination, and therefore we only ever saw the best of her. All our discipline was metered out by Rhoda, with no doubt Mum's supervision, so I can never remember her ever shouting or screaming at us.

It has been difficult to really get close to my brother, Martin, although we have always had a good relationship. He left home at 16 to join the Navy and since then we have had intermittent contact dependent on both his and my current situation. We have kept in touch more often since Mum died. I will always be grateful to him for getting me through the depression and grief I felt at losing Mum. His insights are always refreshing and I often pass on some of his advice to my friends and colleagues.

Here are a few of them:

Give in to the grief, it is a natural process that everyone goes through to some extent!

Don't get rid of anything until at least a year has passed!

Remember only the good times and forget the bad!

I also have a step sister, Maura, and a step brother, Nigel. We lost touch with Maura soon after Mum divorced my step dad, however, Nigel kept in touch with Mum right up until she died. He has lived abroad for the last 40 odd years and has 2 children. Caroline has managed to keep in touch but I think I was too young to bond during the times we saw our step siblings, and like a lot of family the tendency is only to keep in touch if you are the one instigating the contact. Much to my regret I never did and the one chance I did have of seeing Nigel was when I went backpacking with D'Artagnan. We were in Sydney while Nigel and his family lived in Melbourne. We had decided to travel down by train, but when it actually came to it, D'Artagnan was ill due to a reaction to all those injections you have to have when travelling.

GROWING UP

For all the events that you will read about in my later chapters I had a lovely childhood. Brought up in East Africa until 11 years old I tend to remember all the good sunny days rather than the more frightening memories that were there from when I was about 5 years old. Even after that most of the events were more an adventure than something to worry about.

I never met my maternal grandparents although Mum did travel to England to see them soon after her marriage break up.

My Father left us when I was 3 months old so I have no recollection and only a few photos of what he looked like. Most of my history was destroyed by my Mum's jealous 2nd husband.

Mum moved to Eldoret when her in-laws threw her out after my Father left her. The years in Eldoret were great, we lived in several houses over the next few years. Initially staying at The Lincoln Hotel. This was my first real memory and I must have been about 18 months old. A colonial building all white with verandas just made for little children to run around. Our first permanent home was a small bungalow situated in the grounds of the hotel. We had measles and chicken pox here. Although I don't remember a lot about this place we had matching green painted beds with white bedcovers embroidered with elves. Funny the things that do stick in your mind after so many years!

We attended the Highland School and then Hill school in Eldoret although how old I was and which house we were living in remains a haze.

My faint memories of school include writing with nibs and real ink and learning to form our letters and words, no doubt the fun was in getting covered in ink! Learning my times tables by rote which has stood me in good stead throughout my life.

Mum was matron at the Hill boarding school we all attended, although as day boarders. The school itself was strict and I do wonder why our schools don't adopt the same attitude to discipline. Each classroom had a basin and a bar of soap which was administered orally to those children daring to use bad or obscene language. A barbaric but effective way that worked for most of the children. It's no wonder we didn't really swear until we came to England. I think they used a carbolic soap, not something we see too often nowadays but a lesson quickly learnt!

One day I was playing with plasticine in the class, no doubt it was something educational, but I managed to stick a sharp pencil straight through my thumb when trying to put a hole in the model I was trying to form. To this day I still have the scar to remember it.

We attended Sunday school regularly and I loved the stories from the Bible and of course the orange drink and biscuits at the end. We would then join Mum at the Church service. I remember we were asked to read the lesson in Church so we all had to attend elocution lessons so we could do it justice. Although we all spoke well after that you can read about the injustice of it in my Childhood Bullying chapter.

We moved to a bigger house on the edge of Eldoret, it was a lovely house with a porch. It was here that Caroline trapped her finger in the bathroom door. My only real overriding memory of this house was that we played with the girl next-door and it was there when Arnott, my Father, came to visit them. I remember hiding on the top shelf of her wardrobe but had no idea why. After all there was no-one to tell me who he was, but I hid there until I could escape back home.

Our next house was a Railway house. A little wooden house with the kitchen in a separate building with a covered walkway between and a swing in the garden. Caroline broke her arm falling in the storm ditch across the road and I ran into a passing car and bounced right over Martin and ended up in the same storm ditch. Not on the same day I hasten to add! The railway club was down the road where we used to play under the building and Martin hit his head on the iron girders a couple of times. We had a jack Russell dog. It was at this house that Mum married my step father, Norman. We stayed with the Headmaster's family while mum was on honeymoon or rather in hospital after Norman managed to roll the car due to his drinking. Should have been a warning for Mum, but then again it was early days in their marriage, in fact not more than a couple of hours!

You may have noticed that as children we seemed to have our fair share of accidents and although Mum would worry about us she certainly valued the freedom and grounding that our playing and explorations gave us. It is such a shame that nowadays parents are too afraid to let their children out to play for fear of them being hurt or in case they come across some of the more undesirable elements of our society. How can they ever learn to take care of themselves if they are never allowed to experience these things. I know, from being a parent myself, that it is essential you teach your children the rights and wrongs in life or it will be more difficult for them to cope as adults when confronted with awkward or difficult situations.

After mum married Norman we went to live in a bungalow further down the road. This was where Martin had white mice, a parrot and a golden cocker spaniel called Dandy. Unfortunately Dandy was run over by a car and my sister never forgave me for laughing instead of crying. There again I was only about 5 or 6 and just didn't appreciate the enormity of what had happened, especially as Dandy had run back to us after the accident, so really I thought he was OK. I remember the parrot used to talk and Mum would stand on the veranda and call us in for tea. The parrot would then take over the calling until we appeared.

One day Martin had come home with 2 small white mice and cajoled my Mother into letting him keep them. After the usual rules e.g. you clean the cage and feed them, it wasn't long before he had at least 100 and a roaring trade at school as he supplemented his pocket money.

We moved to Tabora in Tanganyika (Tanzania as it is now known) as Norman was a train driver and his job meant the move was necessary.

Our first house was a bungalow with a netted veranda. It was at this house that we had a monkey as a pet, called Chico, and he definitely was a little cheeky monkey. He was such fun and he did save us from a really horrible event. One night two robbers tried to break in to our house and Chico bit them as they put their hands through the wire mesh door. They gave up and went next door where they broke in and woke our neighbours, tied them to chairs and generally frightened the living daylights out of them. Chico got a good reward for that!

Our second house was a first floor flat that had a water tower in garden. I think this was where we had an orchard full of guavas and one day a young girl was found scrumping. When Mum faced up to her she stuck to her guns saying the fruit was on a tree and no-one owns trees! Needless to say Mum gave her a basket of guavas and sent her on her way promising never to steal again. She still went away sure in her own mind that she was not stealing. Still I don't remember her coming back again so maybe Mum did get through to her. It was at this house that at night Chico was chained to the outside stair banister that gave him plenty of running room, however, he managed most mornings to unhook himself. Unfortunate for us that he did this at the chain end and not the collar end as he would scamper across our corrugated tin roof at some ungodly hour and wake us all up. Cheaper than an alarm clock I suppose.

One game was a favourite for all 3 of us, Martin would be Tarzan, Caroline was Jane and need you ask who was typecast as the monkey!

I remember how funny it was when the cook/house boy decided to kill a chicken for dinner. He would lay it on a block of wood and chop off it's head, which he was hanging on to, and then the chicken's headless body would fall to the ground, get up and start running round the yard. I am sure this is not something everyone would say was a good experience or even funny, but when you are young and this is a normal way of living, you learn early on that it is necessary if you are living off the land and keeping chickens. I wonder if that is where the saying 'running round like a headless chicken' comes from?

We also had chameleons as pets, these fascinating reptiles change colour depending on the background they are sitting on. A very effective defence mechanism. They are not the sort of pets that run around, moving one leg at a time, in between surveying its surroundings before daring to move the next leg. However, one of the most fascinating things about the chameleon is that when dropped or in shock it turns black. Martin had many a fun day coming into the kitchen, where the servants congregated, dropping his chameleon on the floor and running away. This was followed with screams and a quick exodus from the kitchen! I asked my Ayah why the servants ran away when the chameleon turned black and this was the story she told me. Whether PC or not here it is: Many millennia ago an African tribe decided they wanted to be white, so they decided to send a messenger to God and ask him how they could do this, choosing the chameleon. As I have mentioned the chameleon moves very slowly, so it was some many years later that the chameleon returned and told the tribe to go and bathe in a special river and they would be white. Unfortunately when they got to the river it was dry except for a small trickle running down the middle from which they managed to drink after their long journey. They were only able to place the soles of their feet and the palms of their hands in the diminishing water, and to this day, most black people have white soles, palms, and mouths; and hate chameleons which they claim are the devil in disguise, hence the black colour! As a grown up, I doubt very much that this was a true story, but you never know!

We attended a school run by Fathers and Nuns, specifically for children from Goa, and therefore found ourselves to be amongst the few white children attending. There was us three plus the Police Commissioner's 2 children. It was a lovely school and many of our lessons were taken on the verandas or sitting under the trees due to the heat. Every lunch time some of us would congregate under the Mango tree in the grounds, with the boys throwing stones to knock the fruit down. The girls would bring small packets of salt and we would dip the raw mango into the salt before eating it. To this day I prefer raw to ripe mangos.

The Fathers and Nuns took the children out on excursions and the one I remember most was on a boat, fishing. We stopped at a little island and lit a fire, cooked the fish and ate it. Needless to say, this was not filleted, boned fish you see in England and I managed to end up with a load of bones in my mouth, nearly choking. To this day I prefer not to eat fish, boned or otherwise.

It was while we were at this school that a Rally was taking place and all the schools in the area were asked to perform. I remember my dress so vividly, it was in gold satin with a wire round the rim of the skirt and moved beautifully when I danced. I think we did a Scottish reel, which was down to our teacher who was a young Scottish girl. Her name was Carole and she was slim, blond and blue eyed and I think I was a little in love with her!

We saw a lot of interesting things in Africa that we were not likely to see in England. Such as the day we saw a pregnant woman walking along a dusty road with a small child on her back, a bag and a basin. She stopped, keeping the small child where he was, filled her basin with water from the ditch and squatted down to deliver her baby. All on her own, she cut the cord, wrapped the newborn, tied it to her front, emptied her basin and walked off down the road!

An entrepreneur who ran a large shop in town used to put sweets under the counters which were just off the floor enough for us young children to dive onto our stomachs and get as many sweets as we could reach. All sweets being free to the finder. Mum told us years later that he deliberately put the sweets there as all the Mums could do their shopping there uninterrupted by their children. So it was the most popular shop around.

One day we attended an Indian wedding which was absolutely beautiful, the brightly coloured saris and the beautiful sweet meats making this a memorable occasion. Even more so when I realised this was the first time the bride and groom had actually met! Mind you, there wasn't much divorce around, so maybe it is a good idea to commit yourself for life to a stranger. In England it seems not many couples commit to their vows as testified by the amount of couples splitting up with irreconcilable differences. Why don't they work at it anymore? Marriage is after all about compromises in order to make it work. I have more to say on this in my Getting Married chapter.

Most social events were at the colonial Top club where there was a swimming pool. We often spent Sunday afternoons here, helping make egg mayonnaise sandwiches for afternoon tea. It was here that I learnt to swim, with a lot of bribery. Mum was appalled that I would jump from the top (5m) diving board to the edge of the pool, coming up to grab the rail that ran round the pool just above the water line. The bribery involved a bottle of coke for every width I managed to swim! Needless to say I learnt to swim, although not too quickly! Mum played tennis here and they also turned the badminton hall in to a cinema sometimes. I can remember the fun days when we would have games organised, racing horses (toy ones) up and down the hall.

We used to play kiss chase behind the clubhouse with the local boys and girls. When caught you had to go behind a shed and be kissed, however, I loved the chase but when it came to the kissing I sent Caroline in my place. Not sure if she enjoyed this or not. Maybe I was just too young to appreciate the actual purpose of this game!

It was here that I remember my first embarrassing moment. We had all being playing hide and seek and I had managed to squeeze myself into an empty cupboard. When I was found I slid along the floor of the cupboard to get out the door when I managed to get a huge splinter in my bottom. Running crying to Mum, who was in the bar, I was summarily laid across her knee with my knickers round my ankles while she pulled the offending piece of wood out! Come to think of it that wasn't the first time I had this happen to me, only this time I had sat on a bee which stung my bottom. At least this time we were at friends having tea, but I was still summarily laid across her knee, knickers round my ankles!

Our next move was to a caravan at a house by the Top club. The house was being renovated so that was why we were in the caravan. Not ideal with all 4 of us. Mum had left Norman by then. Although I do remember, once we had moved into the house, he came by bringing presents and toys for us, and I was so envious that Caroline got this huge walking talking doll!

One day Mum, Caroline and I were coming home from visiting and Martin had stayed in the caravan, deciding to hide himself. Unfortunately for him, the cupboard only opened from the outside and he was stuck! He was there for some hours as Mum had decided to stop off on the way home to do some shopping. He was in a right state by the time we found him.

Whether in Eldoret or Tabora we had halcyon days of playing outside. We didn't have television or computer games and had to make our own fun. I remember sitting in the dirt making pictures with the leaves from the ferns, and even eating the dirt. A most satisfying sensual taste in my mouth. We rarely wore shoes and just spent most days living in our own fantasy world, playing chase in the maize fields, tying the maize plants together to make tunnels, and putting on our bathers to play outside in the downpours when they came, stamping our feet and splashing each other.

Not wearing shoes brought it's own penalties, not in getting infections or any remembered cuts or bruises, but in the fact that every night our Ayah would scrub the bottom of our feet with a big scrubbing brush and no amount of squirming, giggling or shouting would sway her from her task. Her answer was always the same, wear your shoes! Bath times were always fun with all 3 of us in the bath together. Mind you the minute Rhoda turned her back or left the room Martin would stand up and pee on us! Mischievous as he was, Martin was always there to protect us and stand by us when needed.

Caroline certainly has more memories than I have of actual events and when they occurred and as she says I very much lived in the moment. So my thanks to her for her invaluable input into the many houses we lived in and some of the events that occurred.

When I was about 7 years old we all travelled from Africa to Scotland in an aeroplane when air travel was in smallish aircraft, with good food, boiled sweets and you could go and sit in the cockpit with the pilot. My stepdad absolutely hated flying and panicked every time the stewardess let us children hand out the sweets to the other passengers wearing her hat. He was convinced we would unbalance the aircraft!

Coming to Scotland gave us all our first introduction to a television and to snow! Staying for 6 months we were enrolled in the local school, so very different from the carefree, fun, education we received in Africa. All the teachers seemed to be bad tempered and all the learning was by rote and punishment. The weather was dull and wet most of the time and we had to wear shoes and coats! How I missed the sun although when the snow came, building snowmen and throwing snowballs was a novelty.

We visited the Braemar Games which are held every year. Lots of people in kilts doing funny games and dancing with swords. The journey up there was scary as the road has a sheer drop down one side and coaches were going up and down, which left little room for the cars. Mum was an excellent driver and we kids found it a great adventure, but my Stepdad was terrified and got out and walked.

We lived with my Step Grandma and Grandpa. Grandpa was dying with Stomach Cancer, which I later learned was the reason we were there. All I remember about this was that we spent the day with my two 'Aunties' while the adults visited Grandpa. Not having much experience in looking after 3 small children my Aunties decided to take us to the shop and bought chocolates and Cream Soda mixed with Ice cream. This was lunch! That night, sharing the bed with one of my Aunties, she came back from a night out and bought more chocolate which I promptly threw up all over the bed and my Grandma went mad, not at me, but my Auntie! The other thing I remember and was annoyed about, even to this day, was when I was sent off in a coach with my chocolate buying Auntie for the day, only to discover on my return that my brother, sister and Mum had all gone to a Zoo and there wasn't enough room for me! It's not that I didn't have a nice day, it was just that I felt I had been fooled and missed out on what would have been a better day! Not helped by Martin and Caroline crowing about their day out!

Living with Grandma was her son, my Uncle, who had an accident when he was 18 years old that inflicted him with being a mute. Deaf, dumb and blind. I heard stories many years later that she kept him in a cupboard under the stairs for much of his life as she was so ashamed of him. Although when we were there he had been taught braille and spent the day reading his books. It must have been so terrible for him as he woke some nights screaming. Mum said it was because it must have been awful to dream about the things he had seen before the accident only to wake up to just silence and blackness.

Of course there were times that were not so carefree. The Mau Mau rising came and went with us all sleeping in one bed with a shotgun handy. The Mau Mau Uprising went under various names. It was a military conflict that took place in British Kenya between 1952 and 1960. The conflict was between Kikuyu dominated groups summarily called Mau Mau, the white settlers, and elements of the British Army, including local Kenya regiments mostly consisting of the British, auxiliaries, and anti-Mau Mau Kikuyu.

We returned home one evening from a day out to find blood all over the veranda. Our neighbour told us they had taken our Ayah to hospital with multiple stab wounds. Apparently she was locking up and was approached by the rebels who demanded the key. When she refused they attacked her and it was only the appearance of the neighbour and his gun that scared the Mau Mau off. Lucky for her and us, she survived. Just shows how loyal some people can remain whatever the odds.

Then there was the Congo rebellion with, initially, European refugees streaming off the trains with little or nothing as they escaped the violence. One woman arrived with 3 babies, she had just delivered her own baby when the rebels attacked the hospital and she managed to save 2 other small babies and get to the train.

It was in Tabora that the Congo refugees came streaming through, so packed on the trains you could hardly see the train itself. People getting of the train, most carrying treasured possessions, whether that was a chicken, a bed or chair. Some had escaped wearing nothing, others in their night clothes. Mum and the other families all got together in a railway warehouse and we dished out clothes, food and a bed to sleep in. I remember Mum making us take some of our old toys with us for the children.

The Congo civil war started on June 30, 1960, when Belgium negotiated post-colonial mining rights in declaring an independent Democratic Republic of the Congo (DRC). During the next 5 years of internal conflict some 100,000 people were killed.

Exciting to us children rather than frightening and this was due to my Mother and the way she protected us and continued to do so until she died in 1991.

Moving to England we had a succession of homes, the first being in Brighton, East Sussex. Put into the local schools we all suffered from bullying and this is covered in my Childhood Bullying chapter.

Our next house was in Hove, living in a top floor flat. It was here that we had a boating lake down the road and we all three spent our summers working on the boats for ice cream! Helping people in and out of the boats and generally having a lovely time. Not to mention the free rides we got.

When our landlord died we had to move again and found a flat with a bakery next door. It was here that my step dad came back into our lives and Mum took him back.

Trying to make a go of the marriage we moved to a smaller town and they ran a Grocer shop. We had to move schools and for me this came at just the time I had passed my 11 plus so I attended the local Grammar school.

I had been to a few schools since moving to England and it was at my second school that I met a girl, Paula, who was to become my best friend for the next 6 years. Although I thought we had lost touch I was surprised to find her at the same Grammar school, in the same class, and sitting next to me! You can read more about this friend in my Betrayal chapter.

Due to the problems with my Step Father we moved quite a few times after the shop, but eventually Mum divorced him and we settled in a lovely flat and it was here that I moved and stayed from my teens to 18 years old. Much of my teen years have been covered in my other chapters.

Caroline got married and Mum and I moved out to the country where she had a tied house with her new job. It was here that I completed school, got a job and then had my son.

It's weird that the times lived seemed much longer than the actual years show. It is true that time goes slowly when you are young, speeding up as the years go by when you suddenly find yourself, well, like me!

CHILDHOOD BULLYING

I got my first taste of being bullied when I came to England and attended my first school. All those mouth washings had worked so well that even though we had been brought up with the foul mouth of my step dad, none of us kids swore. We spoke the 'Queen's English' having taken elocution lessons in our formative years.

This apparently was enough to make us stand out from the crowd and all three of us suffered at the hands of the nasty elements that are still prevalent in our schools today. My first experience was being pushed from behind whilst leaning on a barrier, and I ended up on the other side with bruises and scrapes to my face and hands. Needless to say we learnt to swear and drop our 'haitches' very quickly, much to my Mum's annoyance, after all her hard work.

My second taste of bullying, having got over the speech problem, was experienced in my senior school. Having eaten just about everything I could on the ship over to England I was more than a bit 'puppy' fat and gained the name of 'Tank'. Not an easy thing to live with especially in puberty when trying to fit in with the boyfriend/girlfriend stakes.

Dealing with Bullying is never easy especially as you have no choice but to go to school. Never resolved in my first school, but moving to the Grammar school and meeting Paula put a stop to the bullying. Smaller than me, prettier than me, but with that grit that I lacked.

Caroline on the other hand was bullied for a completely different reason and perversely because she was born in Africa. Her hair was pulled, her lunch money stolen, regularly taunted and generally her life at school was no picnic!

The consequences for both of us, however, were the same. Neither of us had confidence in ourselves until very much later in life and school was never a place either of us took pleasure in or excelled at.

Nowadays children are encouraged to 'grass' on their bullies, or stand up to them. Neither of which resolve the issue and more often than not makes things a lot worse. Equally social media has a lot to answer for as this is the main method of communication between children. The tendency is that once a child is bullied on line it very soon leads to others including strangers from just jumping on the bandwagon for a 'laugh'. I feel for the parents of children who have taken the ultimate step and decided to leave this life rather than get through this phase. Parents are often unaware just what their children are suffering. Equally those of the bullies refuse to believe that their little darlings could do such a nasty thing.

Schools are yet to find an effective way to deal with this issue. Removing mobile phones during school time should be a must. I speak from experience having worked in a secondary school for 3 months and the behaviour of a small group of children can stop the learning and teaching process for all involved.

Social studies showing stories of bullying might just make the perpetrators think twice. Unfortunately I have come to the conclusion that the young children of today lack respect for anything and are encouraged through Internet gaming to be immune to empathy or pity.

I have another bug bear that schools are now teaching our children the things they shouldn't know until they are at the age to fully understand the consequences of their actions. Sex was something that was left to the parents to teach at the appropriate age.

So firstly I blame the parents for not teaching them properly on the social graces required to be a decent human being. Secondly the Government who has taken away any options for punishment at school. Finally the age of technology that for some reason finds it so hard to keep the content decent!

I know we need to protect our children and ensure that excessive punishment is not used, however, children through the ages have managed to get through their formative years even though they have received the cane or had their mouths washed out! The law says you cannot hit your children but I am pretty certain that those types of parents still exist in the privacy of their own homes and legislation will not stop it.

There are tell tale signs for any parent if they care to look. Constant excuses for not going to school, not wanting to go out and play after school, sitting for hours on end in their bedrooms with computers, anxiety attacks on certain days, and in the worst cases definite signs of illness e.g. not eating or eating more, loss or increase in weight. You know your child better than anyone, so any change in behaviour should be a warning that something is not right.

There are all types of bullying that we meet in life and my next experience was within the workplace. Sometimes more difficult to deal with as we get older as so many things have to be considered before taking action, so I have added a chapter on Workplace Bullying.

FINDING LOVE

FIRST LOVES

My first love was in Africa and I must have been about 6 or 7 years old. He was a boy called Tony, who had a friend Ray, and both my sister and I spent many glorious days riding on their bicycle crossbars, putting pennies on the train tracks to squash them, sitting up trees singing songs, and playing kiss chase outside the local club while Mum and Dad socialised. Being that bit younger than Caroline and making her do the kissing, it was no wonder that Tony changed his affections and I got Ray as a substitute.

As I grew older and had moved to England surprisingly with all my 'faults' I did have dates, albeit, brief. However, I never got over the fact that I was always the one who was described as "I don't fancy yours much, mate".

Standing alongside Paula, my beautiful 'best' friend, I could only agree with them deep down.

I do remember an incident when I was about 13 and believe it or not I was going out with the 'hunk' at the local youth club. In retrospect he was probably going out with me for a dare! Anyway he stood me up one night and Paula urged me to confront him and give him a good slap round the face. Egged on, this I did, together with an incomprehensive load of drivel that came out of my mouth as I got further egged on by the crowd. I learnt my lesson from this encounter as I received a resounding slap back and got dumped in public! Never done that again.

I suppose the hardest thing to contend with was the attitude towards me by these so call 'boy friends' who thought I may not be the best thing to look at but always worth a try as a sexual plaything. Keeping my legs crossed, and I did, meant that relationships were short, but at least I didn't get known as the local bike as, I learned some time later, Paula was known.

Between the ages of 11 and 12 I took up ice skating and met the dream boat of all dream boats. He was a member of the local ice hockey team, had blond hair and blue eyes. Every Saturday and Sunday I would go to the rink and attempt to skate while never taking my eyes off this gorgeous boy. Unfortunately all the girls had the same feelings as I did. We would all go to the coffee bar next door and spend an hour drinking coffee and larking around. He never did go out with any of the girls and I never did learn to skate. In my dreams I have always been the slim, athletic, beautiful ice skater, it's just unfortunate that in reality I spent most of my time on my rear end! At least I had the fat to cushion the many falls I took.

Paula and I had many close calls and escapades during our friendship. Whenever we wanted to go to an all night party, stay up later than usual or go and stay with someone our Mums wouldn't agree to, we would say we were staying with each other. We did this a couple of times staying out all night, the first being really frightening as we ended up in a block of flats under construction. That was scary, so the next time we hitched up with a couple of lads who said they had somewhere to stay. Innocent as we were, it was a shock to find ourselves in a hay barn. For me it was a night of terror. Paula seemed settled with her fella, however, for me it was a night of trying to keep my legs closed and my clothes on. I am pleased to look back on this night and know that I didn't succumb and it was worth the fight! I never did stay out again.

My early love experiences added to my already deep rooted lack of self-worth which I was to carry through my teens and twenties.

I think it's only as you get older that you can recognise true deep love although from 15 years old until you meet that someone special we all go through what we think is the love of our life.

GROWN UP LOVE

I have definitely had some real disasters and the first that comes to memory is hooking the best looking guy in our circle. I had gone to a house party and unfortunately had drunk a considerable amount of ginger wine mixed, I suspect, with spirits by my so called friends. A laugh for them I am sure, however, on leaving this guy decided to get me home, so we walked out into the fresh air for half a mile down to the train station where I proceeded to throw up. Luckily I did manage to miss covering him, but gone was my chance to impress. Just to end the evening on a worse note was when my Mum met me down the road from our house and proceeded to tick off the guy and then send me home with a flea in my ear. When I saw him next he was a gentleman and I think realising my shame didn't talk about it and unbelievably we were still a couple!

I was going out with a couple of other guys at the time, but following my success in holding on to the latest one, I decided to ditch the other two. Two days later I was dumped and ended up with no-one.

My next, was a real mistake, as I already had my Son, Ian, and although this guy seemed to accept my situation, he was continually unfaithful to me. Besotted, I forgave him time and again and eventually some 2 years later he asked me to marry him and I accepted, not believing my luck. We went straight to the jewellers and he bought me a lovely 'expensive' ring. My choice as I really thought the more he paid the more serious he was. Anyway the ring was too big so it stayed with the jewellers for the week and as it happens he went off for a week with the gang for a festival in Europe. I picked up the ring on the Friday and wore it immediately, so happy and looking forward to his return on Saturday. He did come back and the first thing he said to me was that he had made a mistake and wanted to call off the engagement. Fuming, I gave him a flea in his ear and went back to the jewellers to sell the ring! As if he hadn't done enough damage to my confidence he then returned the following Saturday saying he had made a mistake and could we get engaged again. Like a fool I agreed, and this time it lasted 2 days! I couldn't believe what was happening to me, made easier when I learnt that he had taken another girl abroad with him and that was when he decided he preferred her to me. Unfortunately for me and for him, she turned him down, hence the immediate return to me. It took me many years to get over what he did, but some 20 years later I saw him again and suddenly realised what a 'prat' he was. I had had a lucky escape!

I also went through the 'sugar daddy' stage when Ian was about 4 years old. I met him at the local nightclub, where I was working, and was flattered by his attentions, the presents and the 'S' type Jaguar car he had. He owned several businesses and was some 20+ years older than I was. Unfortunate in a way that Mum accepted the relationship and welcomed him into the family. If she hadn't then I am sure it wouldn't have lasted the 6 months that it did. He was to be the father of my second child.

Then there was the incident of the married man. I had met his wife so went into the affair with my eyes open! Being young and naïve his stories of his wife not understanding him and their relationship was in name only convinced me that I was the love of his life. This was of course the lies of a serial philander. The repercussions of this brief affair could have been worse and I will explain why. It transpired that he had been sleeping with me and several other ladies at the same time including one of my friends. The first I knew of it was when I received a telephone call from his wife accusing me of having an affair with him. My first instinct, as I am sure yours would have been, I denied it all and told her to tell her husband to stop telling lies and that he was fantasising. Thankfully that was the last I heard from her. Unfortunately my friend didn't have the same quick response when the wife phoned her, and she admitted the affair. It didn't end there for her as the wife was the breadwinner and it was evident that her husband would do and say anything she wanted, no doubt so he wouldn't leave the lifestyle she provided and he had become used to. Never did find out her outcome from this but in a way I was thankful I had gone through this. Sounds strange to say it now but if I hadn't experienced this how could I some 45 years later advise my friend's daughter who had managed to get herself in the same position.

She told me about this married man she had been seeing for some months. I said to her "Don't tell me, let me tell you, he is going to leave his wife but not yet as she is pregnant with his second child, they don't sleep together anymore, and he loves only you". Shocked, she asked me how I knew he had said that? We had a long discussion about married men in general and the reasons they are unfaithful to their partners. In his case, his wife was pregnant and he wasn't getting any sex and once that resumed he was highly unlikely to leave her. Thankfully she saw sense and an event that happened the following week just confirmed our discussion and she gave him the heave-ho!

It is a real shame that as young girls we are so easily manipulated, believing ourselves to be in love, and it is only when you get older and wiser that you can see through all the rubbish and can see these philanderers for what they are!

It took me a long time to get any confidence in myself and that was wholly due to the choice I made with the actual love of my life, D'Artagnan. It was he who has built that confidence in me, giving me unconditional love, and appreciating who I am. He is the best decision I ever made in my life!

Definitely worth going through all those other 'mistakes' so that you can appreciate a good thing when you find it.

BEING A SINGLE PARENT

G etting pregnant at the age of 17+ was not exactly expected, but there again I was practically engaged to a really dishy bloke who besides being my sister's husband's best friend was also the son of a farmer. Our relationship seemed solid and we were talking marriage, to the extent that his Dad was going to give us a piece of land to build a home as an engagement present. All seemed to be heading towards me becoming a farmer's wife, that was until I told him I was pregnant and this must have scared him rigid as he quickly disappeared from our lives even before our son Ian was born. Being young and naïve the thought of being a farmer's wife sounded so romantic and lovely, but in retrospect I think I had a lucky escape!

Unfortunately for me 2 things happened which were to affect my life from then on, with decisions being made on my behalf. Firstly the news of the pregnancy was greeted by both my Mother and Doctor with 'oh well, no use crying over spilt milk'. Why wasn't I offered a choice or alternative? I certainly was when I found myself pregnant again some 2 years later when I opted for an abortion. Don't get me wrong I love my son as most Mothers' do, but what would my life have been like if I had been given some choices?

I don't advocate abortion as being a good thing, to this day I still wonder what my daughter would have been like and grieve for her. That day was so surreal, dropping Ian with my Sister for the day and night and then driving myself to this old Victorian building. They were very good, talking with me first to ensure that I knew what I was doing, then giving them the money they wanted. £200 in those days was a lot, but I had worked hard and used my savings. I just didn't think it right to ask either my Mother or my Sister to fund such a thing. I was taken down to the operating theatre by a jovial male orderly. The next thing I remember was waking up crying and this just didn't stop until the next morning. For all the trauma, not being able to pin down who the father was this time, it was the best decision for me at the time.

My son, Ian, was just such a lovely baby with dark hair and deep brown eyes. In those days hospitals kept you in for a week, giving you time to learn how to feed and bathe a newborn so that by the time I came home I felt everything was just so natural. Mum was a great help and we continued living with her until Ian started school when he was 4 years old.

I have such lovely memories of Ian growing up, learning to walk around the furniture, there was no stopping him. One day I had just got him all dressed up in his nice blue and white sailor suit and left the room for just a minute only to return to find him sitting in the coal scuttle eating the coal! Black smudged all over him and his clothes! Then there was the day we were in the garden and he was about 2 years old and decided, when my back was turned, to take himself off down the road pushing his cart full of toy bricks. I suppose he remembered the walk as we did it every day down to the local shop. What a panic we had searching the garden, never occurring to us that he would have left it. Suddenly I spotted him about 100 yards down the road on the pavement, bare feet, nappy and t-shirt, happy as anything.

We have spent many happy years walking and playing out in the countryside or down the beach in the Summer. We would regularly go to the local woods where I found a huge tree and named it the fairy tree. I would hide treats in the hollow trunk and take Ian and his cousins up there. Their faces were a sight to behold when they found all these goodies left by the fairy. Of course only if they had been good! Not only do Ian and his cousins remember the tree, but also their children, who have also spent time in those woods!

I remember once taking Ian to the local park and he had his favourite Teddy in tow. The one in the picture. Unfortunately we left Teddy there, and that night while Mum was babysitting and I was working at the Nightclub, she called to say Ian just couldn't get to sleep without Teddy. There I was at 1 o'clock in the morning scouring the park, of course no sign of Teddy, so I went to the local police station to report him missing. You should have seen this young bobbies face, as it was his first night on the desk, he really thought his mates were playing a joke on him. Eventually, he agreed to take down Teddy's details, yellow and white wearing a red and white tee shirt and red shorts. We never did find him.

To watch Ian grow up has been the greatest pleasure in my life and the closeness we had when he was young was what I missed most as he struggled from the age of 9 to accept the ready-made family I presented him with.

I took both Ian and Lisa to learn how to ride a horse when he was 12 and she was 9 years old. Both were naturals, and for 6 months we all had lovely weekends, coming to an end when the cost was just too much, and both Ian and Lisa naturally turned their interests to other things.

As Ian got older D'Artagnan would take him out hunting with their air rifles. It was only much later that I found out they weren't up there shooting at wild life, but playing soldiers and shooting at each other! On the understanding of course that they weren't allowed to actually fire directly but as close as possible so they could hear the pellet fly past! Ian has always had an infinity with the land and wildlife and at the age of 15 owned several Ferrets which he took with a friend hunting in the woods in the early hours of the morning. It was a great shock to Ian when diagnosed with epilepsy his friend dropped him like a hot potato. I don't think he ever got over that.

I wouldn't say I was a natural mother, but then who is at 18 without a manual. I tried hard to work to provide for my son and this was, I realise now, a mistake. I should have sat at home on benefits and spent more time going to school events, watching football and generally being there for my son. I missed so much of his growing up as I palmed him off on babysitters and family so I could work. Even holidays he spent with my Mum, sister and her children as I stayed home working. It was only when he was 18 that I found out just how much he resented me for this.

At the age of 15 he was diagnosed with epilepsy and went completely off the rails, skipping school and generally behaving like a moron, actually he was just behaving like all teenagers with the added health problem that would deprive him of his ambition to join the Paratroopers. At 18 he left home, or rather was asked to leave, ended up living with drug dealers and the inevitable happened with the drugs, cannabis mainly, leaving him psychotic.

During the early years of him leaving home I funded his request to go to college, spending the money on books and keeping him. This lasted less than a term as his drug use became more and more his way of life. When he first left home I found him a job working at the local Airport bar and due to a change of management he ended up as bar manager. All he had to do was turn up at 07:30 to unlock the doors. Unfortunately, due to the drugs his lethargy and attitude to his job meant he lost it. D'Artagnan then took him into his business and taught him a skill, which he threw away at the first stumbling block he encountered. Since then he has not worked and is now 47 years old!

I moved him from town to town, flat to flat, spending money to ensure he had the furniture, food and heating. I would call at his flat each weekend to take him shopping, do his housework and washing, and then in the later years phoning him each weekend and taking round milk and money to see him through. Not a good idea as money was spent on cannabis and he gave the food away to get the drugs when he didn't have any money. Eventually I gave up on giving him money and swallowed my guilt!

I stood by him and was there for him whenever he needed me until he was in his late 30s at which time I gave up and put him in the care of professionals.

My Doctor agreed to see him and was in agreement that Ian was verging on psychotic, even I was shocked at the voices he said he was hearing. The doctor decided to sort out Ian's epilepsy first off, and this took about 7 months to actually get an appointment. The first one he missed and I took him to the second appointment some 3 months later. The specialist decided there was nothing he could do unless Ian took his pills, and he was not prepared to retest him as the pills would give a false reading. What pills, I almost screamed! He's not taking his pills and hasn't for some years? The consultancy ended with a strong warning from the Specialist to take his pills. So no help there then!

Back to my doctor who had promised to deal with Ian's psychosis once the epilepsy had been sorted. My doctor refused to see Ian saying he was not his patient. So back to square one again. It was fortunate in a way that Ian's psychosis was to eventually lead to him being sectioned. Not that that worked either.

If only I had done this when he was 16/17 and maybe he would have had a chance, but I didn't and my sadness and regret continues every day for my lack of ability to make his life better than it is today. After many years of heartache Ian still wanders through life like a lost soul.

It was a very sad time for us all when Ian was sectioned. I had received a phone call at 2am telling me that the police had been called to his flat as he was throwing things through his fourth floor window. The police doctor had decided, after being told by Ian that he had a snake as a pet and couldn't find it, that he was having hallucinations! No way was I going to tell him that the snake did exist and had somehow managed to escape and was no doubt living under the floorboards! The next call I received was from the Police saying that Ian had walked out of the flat and no-one had stopped him, and that now no-one knew where he was. After a sleepless night I called the police to see if they had found him and where he was now. They had apparently found him wandering the streets and he was now located at the local Psychiatric hospital, where he remained for the next 4 or 5 months.

I was visiting Ian each week and was invited to join his weekly assessment meeting. Ian spoke very little other than to question the doctor's qualifications to diagnose him. At the end of the meeting the Doctor told me that Ian was very ill and it would take months to help him through it. I had a week of feeling a bit of euphoria at the thought that at last there was a chance I would get my son back! The following week I was called in to be told that they wanted to discharge him as he wasn't speaking to them! What happened to the Doctor in a week? Suddenly Ian was ready to be let out into the community again. No amount of sanity could get through to the psychiatrist – surely it was his job to get Ian to talk through his issues? The only thing I managed to do was to ensure Ian did not leave the hospital until his benefits had been sorted out. They were going to discharge him with £9 in his pocket and send him back to his flat. The same flat where he had been beaten, tortured and evicted from his home on a nightly basis by some really nasty drug dealers.

The drug dealers returned within weeks and took over Ian's flat once again. This time I decided enough was enough and called the Police and the Housing Association. Interestingly the police were already watching Ian's flat as they were following the drug dealers, but they were not prepared to evict them. Neither was the housing association, their answer being Ian would have to lodge a complaint. He didn't even know what day of the week it was let alone have the power to stand up to these nasty, so called friends of his.

So leaving Ian downstairs with a neighbour I knocked on the door of his flat. It was evident these two guys had moved in, so I explained that Ian had no right to ask them to stay and that they would need to leave immediately, and I would drive them and their stuff to wherever they wanted within reason. Alternatively they could wait an hour or so when the Police and the HA would evict them and their luggage to the street. I left them for 20 minutes and on my return found them packed and ready to leave and could I drop them at the next town! I agreed and away we went.

Both the Police and the Housing Association wanted to know how I had managed to evict them without any trouble! The Police were only interested in where I had taken the drug dealers!

Eventually Ian moved to a new flat a bit closer to me and we all hoped that this was to be a new start for him. It took just 2 weeks for the drug dealers to find him, no doubt helped by Ian seeking a new supplier for his cannabis. They would follow me and Ian to the post office each week and take £100 for drugs given to him 'on tick' during the week. So the saga continued, with me going round each week to take him shopping and clean his flat, until eventually he started drawing on his walls! This frightened me quite a bit as the drawings were quite explicit about me being raped and beaten. Ian said his friends had drawn the pictures, but whether they had or not, D'Artagnan, and I, worried for my safety.

You read regularly in the papers about psychotic teens killing their parents, and for the first time in my life, I started to believe this could happen. No more visits on my own, and Ian was left in the hands of the Mental Health workers.

To this day he still suffers and lives in his own flat under 'Mental Health in the Community'. He has 6 days of support with carers popping in to help him with looking after the flat and himself, taking him shopping and sometimes taking him out.

For some reason Ian no longer rings me, or answers his phone regularly, he doesn't want anything from me and deters me from going into his flat. The only light in my tunnel is that sometimes when he answers the phone he actually sounds normal and drug free. I cry inside every day.

Marrying my soul mate when my son was 9 was probably another mistake, not for me but for my son, as he never accepted him as his father and fought against him constantly. In retrospect from having me to himself to having to share me, this was the start of his feeling of isolation. Taking on my husband's daughter when she was 7 years old didn't help with the family unit, although I was blissfully unaware of the issues the children were having with each other. My son resented the new addition of my husband and then being presented with a sister who both took the time away from him that he was used to getting as an only child.

Most of our marital rows have been caused by the children. I wanted D'Artagnan to take on the role of Father but neither of them wanted it. He has always been there for my son, putting up with the rudeness and sullenness, giving him a job and training him when he was unable to get work. He was willing to discipline him when he was younger and although that was something I wanted him to do I continued to nag and fight every decision he made that I disagreed with so that eventually he gave up. Who could blame him!

My heart aches every day for my inability to see things as they were rather than as I thought they were or wanted them to be. I continue to blame myself for my shortcomings which have evidently affected both my children in one way or another. The guilt I feel is ever present and no amount of telling myself that these events are past and cannot be changed can take that guilt away.

Ian is a clever, intelligent and good looking boy who could play a mean game of chess at the age of 5. He continues to have all these attributes, I just wish he could see them for himself, rather than hide behind the man he shows himself to be today. I occasionally see my son in him, but most times he is a stranger and I worry for him when I am gone.

FINDING MY SOUL MATE

My soul mate, D'Artagnan has been the one redeeming feature in my family failures. I met him when I was 15 when I was working in a cafe on a Saturday. His fiancée had just thrown her ring back at him, for some misdemeanour on his part, so we decided to teach her a lesson and go out together. With the age difference, him being 18, he collected me from school, helped me with my homework and took me to the local coffee bar. We didn't have any deeper relationship as we both knew the reason why we were together. After 3 weeks the fiancée came back and off he went to marry her and have his daughter.

Our paths crossed now and then as he was a musician and his band played at the Nightclub I worked in, although I was more likely to see him at the local coffee bar. D'Artagnan worked for the Cruise Liners initially and later on moved on to the Merchant Navy. This meant he was away for up to 3 months at a time with a few weeks home in between.

It was to be some 6 years later that he came back into my life, by then divorced from his wife. We started our friendship again. Again he went abroad and this time came back with another girl in tow who he lived with for the next 2-3 years. A few years later we met again and started our friendship again, playing chess, going out to pubs, playing music and generally being soul mates, but no deeper relationship as I was by then quite cautious as to how long he was going to stick around.

During this time he was summarily thrown out from his parents house and came to live with me. I met his daughter and she started to come over every fortnight for visits, and these continued even when he went back to sea. Although I missed him there was a silver lining in my cloud as he left me with his MGB GT daffodil yellow sports car. Boy did I feel great driving around with the top down. The worst thing about leaving the car with me was that he insisted the weekend before going back abroad to adjust the timing/tuning, which worked lovely for that day, however, as soon as he was gone I would have to get the mechanic out to re-adjust it! I didn't bother telling him as the car gave him so much pleasure whether driving it or just tinkling with the engine.

That last weekend before he left he gave me an ultimatum that he wanted more from the relationship or he was never coming back. I must admit that not only did I not want to lose him as a friend I was just as clear in my mind that I did want the relationship to become something deeper. For the next 3 months we exchanged love letters so that by the time he returned we naturally fell into the relationship we both wanted. We had never felt the need to marry, but things were to change when we took on custody, care and control of his daughter.

GETTING MARRIED

L ike the majority of women, we all want to look back at our wedding day, with photos, super dress, loving family around us, the cars, the cake, the limo. Our wedding was so very different and remembered for so many different things.

Following the court case for custody of his daughter, we found ourselves sitting in the local registry office waiting to see the registrar. It was a hot sunny day and we just chatted aimlessly about honeymoons, thinking of going to see his brother in South Africa. This led to the reception and who would be coming, who would expect to come, and who we would actually like to be there. The list just grew and grew when all we wanted was a piece of paper and to leave out all the pomp and circumstance. By the time the registrar came out and asked if he could help us we both just said no at the same time, and decided that we would elope to South Africa and get married without telling anyone. Although we told the kids we would have a secret to share with them when we got home.

So we parked the kids with the grandparents and flew off for 5 weeks and had a lovely honeymoon, getting married 2 days before we came home, at the local magistrates court.

My wedding certificate looks like a supermarket receipt and is written in Afrikaans and has subsequently been destroyed in a flood, so I only have a photocopy now!

The holiday began with a trip to the lawyers to arrange a pre-nuptial agreement. This was because women were not allowed to own anything in South Africa unless the agreement was in place. So should we ever return to SA I will own everything! Not sure in these modern times whether that law has changed.

We had decided to marry wearing our jeans which suited us both. However, my sister-in-law spent the preceding weeks taking me shopping and trying to get me to buy a 'decent' dress.

This was not what we wanted and on the morning of the wedding, instead of getting ready D'Artagnan sat patiently on the bed while I tried on everything I had in my case or had been cajoled to buy. Only when I put on my jeans did he start getting dressed. A wise man, even then. I sometimes wonder if this should not have warned him just what a difficult woman I was. In fact, when the magistrate came we were asked to sit at the back and she was going to marry our witnesses instead who were, as the judge saw it, appropriately dressed! Putting her straight we were married almost before I realised. I thought she was doing the usual chat about the legalities when suddenly she said we were married. I had missed it all! Outside we took photos of a mixture of 3 f us together at a time and then asked a passing stranger to take a couple of the four of us. A good idea, but in those days you didn't know if the photo was any good until you had the film developed. Which we did in England only to find that the one picture of the 4 of us was blurred and cut off the top of our heads! I now have 2 wedding photos which hang on the wall in our downstairs toilet. My in-laws have spent many years taking 'decent' photos of us whenever we attended someone else's wedding!

After the 'ceremony' we all went to a hotel for a roast beef sandwich and a whisky, only to be summarily thrown out for wearing Jeans. My in-laws went back to work and D'Artagnan and I went home, sealed our commitment in the most personal way, and then donned our swim suits and spent the afternoon sunbathing on the President's lawn. I should mention that my in-laws apartment was just across the road from the Government building in Pretoria. We hadn't actually had an invite but it was OK and we actually watched a full white wedding group posing for pictures in the lovely grounds. If only I had known our pictures weren't going to turn out so well I should have got a couple of our honeymoon! Although I don't think I can count on the one of us dressed in fancy dress on New Years' Eve. I was a pirate and D'Artagnan went as a mafia don!

Just as an aside, D'Artagnan and I went shopping just before Christmas and bought our wedding rings which we wrapped and gave to each as presents, much to the disgust of our in-laws who felt we were not taking our wedding seriously enough. No amount of telling that we only wanted the piece of paper for the courts so that Lisa could stay with us would deter them from their thoughts on the subject.

Flying back we were greeted by our families and the two kids jumped over the barriers at arrivals, running up to us shouting "Are you married Dad, are you married Mum"? There were a few smiles and titters coming from the wider waiting audience at the barriers. What a lovely end to a super honeymoon/wedding.

Although eloping did mean that his Father did not speak to us for nearly a year for daring to go and do this dastardly deed without his consent. I hadn't realised that I was expected to ask for D'Artagnan's hand in marriage!

I did manage to go to a proper wedding when we were there, and the dress my sister-in-law had insisted I buy, was just ideal. The funny thing about it all was that we travelled in the car with the bride, who we had just met that day, and as my Brother-in-Law got lost it was a big rush when we arrived at the Church. So much so that I found the bride hanging on to me almost down the aisle while people took photographs. I often wonder if she still looks at her wedding photos and asks herself "Who is that woman"?

Married Life

I don't pretend that married life has been perfect as so much depends on what is going on around you, whether it be work or family.

As husbands go, and from what I have seen for myself from other relationships, D'Artagnan is the best any girl could wish for. When we were presented with the ultimatum of taking on his daughter or allow her to live in a Muslim country and be brought up as a muslin, our lives were to change dramatically.

We were living in a Council House and with the addition of his daughter we needed to move. The Government of the day were offering the sale of council houses at a fraction of the price. So out we went and chose a 3 bedroom property and moved as soon as we could. D'Artagnan was working driving parcels round the country at the time, so he was out all night and slept all day. The children, during the move, were away at alternate weeks camping. So Lisa helped with the packing and Ian helped with the settling in. I did all the moving of everything I could in the car and woke D'Artagnan on the Saturday morning to help me move the heavy stuff. By Sunday we were in! I think it took months before the family knew where I had put everything.

Life has never been easy for D'Artagnan having gone through multiple depressions, mine of course, several operations, mine again, an ectopic pregnancy and the menopause, again mine, although there has been evidence over the last year or two of him suffering depression and possible male menopause. I have to keep telling myself that his patience has to be mirrored by mine.

He has proved faithful throughout the years, although like many possessive wives I spent our early years looking for trouble. Convinced to the point of paranoia that he couldn't possibly be faithful to someone like me. I must have made his life hell, continually checking his mobile, pockets and of course with the inevitable arguments.

Once you have in your head that your husband is going to be unfaithful, nothing he says or does will convince you. I don't suppose it helped that the technicolour dreams I was having during that period were very real and it was these that I was experiencing so no wonder D'Artagnan was so bewildered as I questioned him on his comings and goings. Even knowing that he had not had the opportunity to be unfaithful did nothing to dispel these nightmare happenings. It has only been for the last 10 years that I have realised that looking for trouble makes you miserable, so why not wait until it actually happens. Trust is so important and it took me a long time to realise that the freedom I have to live my own life and make my own decisions comes from his inherent trust in me.

Thinking about his life, it cannot have been easy for him to watch me work in a succession of jobs where the majority of co-workers are male and not once has he questioned me or bought any fears he might have into the open.

I have always been amazed that he is still with me as I have been and probably still am a volatile person to live with. As he once said, one day he comes home and puts his paper down on the table and the next day I shout at him for doing the same thing. During our marriage he has left me several times, and who could blame him. Each time this happened I realised that my life without him would be unbearable and thankfully he returned. He must have been walking on egg shells for most of our married life. Although now that I am on the happy pills I think deep down D'Artagnan misses the old volatile me.

I suppose we all do it when we get married, we spend 16+ years giving all our time to the children and the house and expect our husband to do his own thing. As we already had children we never had that blissful time together as a couple without all the trials and tribulations that come when children and families become such a major part of your lives. Suddenly in your forties the children leave home and you are told to do your own thing. What is my own thing? I didn't have any hobbies, other than teaching yoga once a week. He was playing out in the evenings with his band and I would be left at home watching television or spend endless evenings sitting on my own in a pub or club. Jealous if I didn't go and fed up if I did.

The answer for us came with a 3 month tour he got in London for his 10 piece soul band and his sound engineer decided he couldn't spend the time. So before I knew it, and after 20 minutes on a 24 channel mixing desk, I found myself in London learning on the job. I think the best time I had was when D'Artagnan decided to put together a Pink Floyd tribute band. 13 people on stage and all connected to my new 32 channel desk! The music was sublime and every evening I spent, whether in a pub or a theatre, was just heaven! Having a shared interest was the answer for us and for the next 20 years we have spent every evening together, whether it is out with the band or just flaking at home.

Taking in Jemima, his Mother, when she got divorced was a definite change in our lifestyle. Not so much in the first 5 years of her living with us, but as her age and dementia have taken their toll we find ourselves as restricted as having a new born baby! The time for going out and playing live music came to an end as D'Artagnan didn't think it was fair that I should remain at home to look after Jemima just so he could carry on. I have tried during these years to encourage D'Artagnan to follow his love of playing live music and not to worry about me. There will come a time when I will be free and in the meantime he can continue trying to put a band together and rehearse as much as he wants. Between bands he decided to try and go out as a solo performer and I absolutely love listening to him playing at home. He is not only a phenomenal guitar player but also plays a mean keyboard.

Besides music one of our shared pleasures was having dogs! Not that I anticipated having more than one. We started when the kids were about 10 and 12, and we had decided that we would not have any more children. So we bought a lovely all black, long haired German shepherd and we settled down to sorting out our position in his life. For the purposes of this book I will call him Darth Vader! D'Artagnan was the master and undertook all his training, I was the Mother, feeding machine, and the one he would run to when he was frightened or hurt, Ian was always good for a rough and tumble and if he just fancied a cuddle or fuss then Lisa was his favourite. He was such an intelligent dog and learnt very quickly so that all instructions could be off the lead with hand signals or special words. We all spent many a happy hour taking Darth out for his many walks, and he quickly learnt to play frisbee, hide and seek, tobogganing in the snow and became an integral part of the family. Not that the children would ever take him out for walks, but then it wasn't their decision to have a dog in the first place! The good thing about a dog, especially a large one, is that twice a day you have to give them the exercise they need and consequently both D'Artagnan and I got a lot fitter during those years.

We have so many lovely memories of those years, some that make me cringe a bit even now! Especially the day we went round to the garage with Darth in the back seat and while after looking in the garage and chatting we got back in the car and drove 3 miles to the in-laws only to find when we opened the back door, no Darth! In a state of panic, well I was, D'Artagnan rushed back to the garage, but he was not there! He drove slowly down the route home and found him sitting patiently at the front door! One smart dog!

I always felt safe with Darth protecting the whole family. If he was off mooching round the park and someone approached me then Darth would be by my side in a flash just waiting for the command to attack if necessary. D'Artagnan had taught Darth to attack on command, but unfortunately he would only go for D'Artagnan and no-one ever gave us the opportunity to try it out on a stranger! Lucky I suppose. For all his bravery, Darth at home would still bark at anyone coming to the door, but as they entered so he would back up the stairs, barking as he went.

One day we were on the beachfront playing hide and seek with Darth, when I went to hide behind a beach hut. Suddenly there he was racing towards me, then just flew over the wall behind me. As his front legs hit the top of the wall he realised there was a 20 foot drop the other side, but he had too much impetuous to stop and much to the surprise of the golfers below, landed on his feet, stunned, but luckily no further damage. No more playing hide and seek there again!

Our second dog to join the family was a rescue Blue Rhone German shepherd. Although she was a difficult dog, you could understand it when you saw the damage that her previous owners had done to her. Broken ribs, teeth kicked out, leaving her with a general feeling of anxiety. She had a strange antipathy towards old women in long rain macs and would run hell for leather towards any that she saw. She also attacked little dogs and would run across the park towards them. One day I saw this man holding his terrier above his head as she jumped to get to it. She, I shall call her Leah, and Darth got on well together over the next few months and even our cat accepted this new member of the family. The amazing thing was that both dogs loved chasing cats and when out walking in the morning around the block, Tina would join us, winding her way through the dogs legs whilst they were eagerly looking for cats! I had convinced both dogs that Tina was a Tina and not a cat.

They are amazingly intelligent animals. One night Darth was chewing a beef bone in the kitchen and once we were in bed we heard him come up the stairs and lay down at the top, chewing away. Very quietly D'Artagnan told him that was not acceptable and he should take the bone back downstairs. After a few moments we heard Darth utter a big sigh as he picked up his bone and took it downstairs where he promptly threw it on the kitchen floor and grunted his disapproval.

The funniest thing that happened, although it didn't feel like it at the time, when Leah came into 'heat'. Darth would guard her as he had been told that he was not allowed to mount her. Believe it or not he never attempted it. One day, while out walking, the biggest Great Dane I had ever seen decided he was interested in Leah and we almost ran home to stop Darth attacking him. First sign of this was when we found the Great Dane sitting in our car, having heaved himself in through an open window. Another time I got in the car with the dogs and the Great Dane ran down the road after the car. We must have looked a real sight with Darth barking like mad in the back and Leah trying to get out the small crack in the window. Thankfully the Great Dane gave up before I reached the main road, otherwise I have no idea how I would have dealt with him.

The saddest time was when Darth got spondylitis and lost the use of his back legs and ultimately lost control of his bowels. He was such a proud dog, so rather than put him through the ignominy of being put on wheels we and the vet decided he should be put down as he would only get worse. The Vet visited us at home, and I hate to think about it now, but somehow Darth knew something very wrong was happening, and D'Artagnan and I had to hold him down while he was being injected. I can still see his soulful and then soulless eyes as he drifted away. So sad! Why is it that losing an animal seems to hit us harder than losing a relation. Anyway, we decided to take him to a special animal rescue place where we could lay him to rest. A big mistake, having put Darth and Leah in the car, we arrived to be told to drive to a special building where we were instructed to put him in, what looked like a dumb waiter. We had to re-arrange his body so that we could fit him in. I hated leaving him there and regret that decision to this day. Leah joined Darth some six months later when she died of kidney failure.

We didn't replace our dogs as by then his Mother Jemima had moved in with us and at 80 years old we were concerned that any size dog was likely to knock her over. However, once Tina grew old and died we did replace her with another rescue cat, Petie, and he has been an absolutely lovely cat. The house seems so empty when you are so used to being greeted by an animal.

Animals love D'Artagnan, especially wild birds. He has found so many carrion birds over the years who have been hurt or damaged in some way. He brings them home and cares for them, releasing them back to the wild when they are ready.

Birds, from my point of view, are very different from the dogs. Let me explain... Once I had a seagull who was suffering from botulism living in my bathroom for six weeks. I would find myself sitting on the toilet in the morning hand feeding fish to the bird as it sat on the edge of the bath! Next there was the Raven. He was only a baby and D'Artagnan fed and watered him as he grew up. Next was teaching him to feed himself and then eventually he needed to learn to fly. One of the funniest sights I have ever seen is D'Artagnan running round the streets with the Raven on his shoulders, holding on for dear life, and learning to flap his wings! I have no doubt this strange sight gave the neighbours something to talk about. Once he was confident enough with his wings, he suddenly just lifted off and was gone. No doubt there will be lots more birds for my Saint of wild birds to save.

Just a tip on Ravens – they constantly go to the toilet, all over the floor, the stairs, the carpet, the lounge suite. By the time he had gone we had to renew everything! I must say that our carpets and furniture were due for a change, otherwise I am not so sure I would have been so tolerant. As for being pets, they are the most friendly and loving animals and this one became part of the family very quickly.

Rows are something that are inevitable within any relationship and ours is no different, although we both realise that most of our rows are caused by other people, the children, the family, or money. Over the years I think we have both learned to hold our tongues and think twice before berating each other for something.

I have become convinced that male and female are actually two different species with sex being the one thing that makes a marriage work. The rest you have to work on. Men don't see the washing up, or the mess around the house, but if you ask them to carry out any chore they will do so willingly, provided of course you allow them to do this in their own time! If you can't wait then do it yourself without blaming him. Do it in your own time, when you feel like doing it.

The only thing I will say about rows, is don't go to bed without making up, hug and kiss regularly and think before you speak, once said it is very hard to undo or take it back.

Sex as I have said is important and he has suffered a lack of this intermittently over the years due wholly to my moods rather than his. Being too tired after looking after the kids or working, being paranoid about his faithfulness and depriving him deliberately, or as of late being on anti-depressants. One of the worst things you can do as it diminishes your sex drive completely. D'Artagnan understands this and is very loving and accepting and has in fact encouraged me to continue taking the happy pills as he just can't bear to see the depths of depression and emotional outbursts recent work and home pressures have put on me.

It was lovely last year when we decided to get married again, primarily as I had managed to destroy my marriage certificate. Thought we might just have the white wedding and all the hoo-ha this time round. However, our hopes were dashed when we were told we would be breaking the law if we did. Somehow renewing our vows was not as appealing as we renew our vows every day we are together.

In fact we have a pact that when it is time for one or both of us to leave this life we have together, then we will make this move together. A sunny beach, our love, and drifting off with the tide after a cocktail of drugs. Either that or a true viking funeral! I think I would prefer to be burnt than have the fishes feast on my remains.

Being retired now we are both determined to try to live our lives as fully as we can and are fit and able to do so. The first thing will be an extended holiday and then maybe travel, staying in different countries for a reasonable length of time until we find a place we would like to see out our remaining years. Of course while Jemima is with us, our plans are just wishful thinking. In the meantime we are preparing the house so we can let it out while we are away.

This job is enormous after 35 years of living here, but we have managed to clear the shed and garage and we are working on the loft! Although there does seem to be the problem of clearing the garage then filling it up again with stuff from the loft, and of course vice versa. Hopefully it will all resolve itself. I set myself a goal every week to do out a cupboard or wardrobe while D'Artagnan does the heavy work outside.

My personal plan is to have everything sorted so we can escape as soon as possible.

D'Artagnan and I were friends long before we were lovers and I really believe that this is the answer to a successful and life long relationship. Whatever has come between us during our time together we neither of us want to lose our best friend!

The consequences of my choice to be with D'Artagnan were definitely unforeseen but we have both worked hard to keep our friendship and marriage together whatever life throws at us!

When I first met D'Artagnan he always had about £400 in his back pocket, lovely blond hair and a bright yellow MGB GT sports car. I often wonder why he gave all this up to be with me!

I have never regretted the choice I was given to either consolidate my relationship with D'Artagnan or let him go. This was one of the best decisions I ever made in my life.

STEP CHILDREN

Taking on a step child, whatever the reason, can be very difficult and needs careful consideration to the affect this can have, especially when the family unit is already settled and working!

The mother of D'Artagnan's child became the bane of my life for the next 10 years. We had certainly had difficulties with the access arrangements which were one weekend every fortnight. Lisa was always the one to suffer from her Mother's erratic lifestyle, endless boyfriends and her drinking. She hated Lisa coming to me and made her life very difficult, haranguing her after every visit and making her feel guilty for actually enjoying herself. Eventually, she decided to go and live her own life in a middle eastern country and bring Lisa up as a Muslim. When she was refused permission to take her she decided to dump her and I was asked if I would be willing for her come to live with me. Bearing in mind that for the most part D'Artagnan would be abroad working I still said yes as by then I felt we had a built a good relationship between us and Lisa took it in her stride and was happy to stay with me and her Father. Her fortnightly visits to me continued even when D'Artagnan was away.

The court cases - although I had agreed to take Lisa on her Mother still insisted on going to court to make things legal. Care and Control was signed over to D'Artagnan even though the case took place while he was abroad, but with glowing reports from her Mother on what a good Mother I was and that she had no qualms about leaving Lisa with me the judge signed the order.

I think this first 6 months was the happiest we had as a family, Lisa felt no stress or abandonment, and settled down well. During this period of time her Mother didn't even ring to see how Lisa was settling down. As we had no idea which country she was in there was no way we could contact her, even in an emergency. To me, this just showed how much, or rather how little, Lisa meant to her Mother. Occasionally Lisa would ask why she had not heard anything, but being 7 years old, it was easy to distract her from worrying too much about the lack of contact.

Much to our surprise and with no warning some six months later her Mother returned to England and contacted us to get Lisa back. D'Artagnan and I had a talk with Lisa, involving the social services at the same time, and it was clear that Lisa did not want to return to her Mother. So she went back to court to get Lisa back. We realised that this was more due to the fact that with a daughter she could get a council house and without her she couldn't. So back to court we went, again without D'Artagnan, and this time I was the Mother from hell. Luckily for us we had continued the court protection order and involved the social services. The order had been placed on her Mother when D'Artagnan was working abroad as Lisa's life with a drunken mother was difficult. Sometime later Lisa had to be placed in foster care, having been abandoned by her Mother, temporarily living with her Grandparents and had contracted Impetigo. After hospital care D'Artagnan's Father would not have Lisa back in the house and as D'Artagnan had to return to work and was unable to care for her full time Foster carers was the answer.

Annoying as Social Workers can be and the troubles that they can cause, it was their reports that made the judge decide to give Lisa back to her father even though we were still unmarried and I was of course a single mother with a 9 year old son.

We had more trouble getting hold of a rescue dog when we already had a dog!

It took a couple of years to get Lisa back to being a child, make her healthy after years of neglect, and to ease her thoughts from her turbulent past. It was a surprise to her that she was not expected to clean the house and do the shopping but just to play and enjoy life.

She was always an independent soul and the continued influence of her Mother during her fortnightly visits kept her from fully integrating with the family. In fact over the years of family get togethers it was always a welcome surprise if she attended or stayed longer than 5 minutes!

The family got used to this behaviour and Lisa was never made to feel uncomfortable by anyone other than perhaps me and her own guilt.

Lisa left home at 17 after an argument with her Father about early nights when she was at College, and living within the house rules. I implored her not to go but to wait until she had completed her education however she was adamant. I helped her move as much as she would let me. Over the years Lisa has excluded me as much as possible from her life and that of her son, my grandson, and although I have tried over the years to be there for her she continues to put up barriers. Putting up with the hurt of having to book my grandson 3 weeks ahead, her evident dislike of my family, and the fact that she always introduces me as her Father's wife, have taken their toll. Turning the other cheek, being the adult, is not always easy, but over the years we have managed in turns to be civil or great friends. I have always been there for her, helping her move house when asked, decorating her house when she was 8 months pregnant, and generally tried hard to keep contact with her and keep them in the family unit over the years since she left home.

Unfortunately some 5 years ago, out of the blue things changed dramatically when she sent a text message to me saying she hated me and never wanted to see me ever again and I was to delete her number and she would do everything she could to ensure I had no influence on my grandson ever!

Apparently I was using emotional blackmail and she had had enough. The emotional blackmail was because I was trying to get her to visit her Nan before her dementia got any worse and she completely forgot who her granddaughter and great grandson were! So I hold my hands up to that but even I hadn't realised that sending her a text and asking her if she would like to join us for a coffee or trying to lend her £7K to start up a business constituted emotional blackmail. You learn something new every day!

I would love to rectify our relationship but if I do, this will conflict with D'Artagnan's wishes and I don't want to lose everybody. One day maybe she will grow up and want to come back into my life. My only wish is that it happens sooner rather than later, having missed so much of my grandson's formative years, I have just discovered through facebook that I am a great grandmother! Whatever she said to my grandson was enough to keep him away from us, although we continue to hope that he will want to have us in his life at some stage.

For all the trouble with her Mother and the later problems with Lisa I have never regretted the choice I made all those years ago to include her as part of my family. To see her blossom from the under fed waif with constant black rings round her eyes, to a strong and beautiful woman, is reward in itself. Although Lisa won't admit it to herself, she spent only 3 years out of her first 7 years with her Mother and 10 years with me, and yet today she feels obliged to support her Mother!

I continue every day to be hurt and saddened by these events, but unless Lisa apologises to me, D'Artagnan does not want her in our lives. I do understand, as taking on Lisa changed and disrupted our lives from that day to this, and although he is grateful for what I did for Lisa he finds it hard to forgive her for the sheer nastiness and vitriol I have had to put up with not just from her but from her Mother over the years.

In today's world there are many split and mixed families, some that work well and some that don't. From my experience, it is not until after they grow up and leave home, and you grow up yourself, that you realise you could have handled things so much better than you did. Hindsight is a waste of time as you cannot change what is past, you just have to learn to move forward and try to rectify the issues if you can.

Families! Communication is the main answer, but it does have to be a two way street, and when one party is not interested, you cannot rectify the situation.

IN LAWS

M ost people have issues with their in-laws for one reason or another and my relationship was no different. D'Artagnan's mother, Jemima, and I became friends and his Father hated me. Probably because I could see the abusive way he treated his wife and encouraged her to try and get a life for herself rather than always sitting waiting for him to make decisions for her.

Jemima was brought up in the North of England and had 2 brothers, the eldest dying during WW2 and the youngest serving in the Navy and then living in South Africa, returning to England in his later years and then dying of a heart attack. Her Father died whilst living in South Africa and later her Mother, who after returning to England died of cancer. Unfortunately for Jemima her family decided not to tell her of her elder brother's death and to this day she still searches for him. Her husband kept her away from her Mother during her illness, I am sure to protect her from the hurt, but all it did was wipe it from her memory completely.

She was very unhappy when I first met her and was subdued by her husband. We would go shopping every week and she would attend my Yoga class for the next 30 years becoming one of the most supple of the lot of them. She worked hard at the jobs she was allowed to do and loved being away from the house and having a social life, which she didn't seem to get much of at home.

As she got older and retired she took up voluntary work at the hospital until he made her give it up as he felt she was bringing home bugs that made him suffer. So every ailment he got during that time was blamed on her. As a quiet, unobtrusive sort of person, Jemima would just give in rather than put up with the constant haranguing she got.

She was forever trying to get away from him and did in 1948 after her first son was born and then again in 1965 when her two sons were in their early teens. She escaped to her family but her freedom was short lived. Any letters she sent to her boys were intercepted and unread. Constant telephone calls and eventually a visit with both boys in tow made her return. The third time was after she had been beaten and her colleagues at work found her a flat. Again he found her and harassed her until she returned. Then fourth time lucky her first real chance came when she was 80 years old and once out of the house we could not get her to go back, although I did try to get her involved in marriage counselling. Unfortunately her younger son and his wife and Lisa convinced her to get a divorce. Of course no offer of help to go down this route.

This meant that the whole process was left for me and D'Artagnan to deal with. A very fraught and difficult time for us to deal with the fall out, 4 years of solicitors and anxiety attacks for Jemima as she tried to cope with his unexpected visits to the house almost daily. Lisa had promised to look after her Grandad as he wouldn't have anything to do with us and with his subsequent death a year after the divorce it became apparent that this promise had not lasted very long, leaving him to drink and smoke himself to a heart attack. Both D'Artagnan and I regret this happening, but what do you do when you are not made aware until it is too late? If only I had been aware that she was not supporting him I would have been pushy and at least got his shopping done for him. I suppose at that time I was overwhelmed with trying to work full time and deal with Jemima.

During those 4 years Jemima would cringe in fear behind the door whenever he visited us. Anxiety and a brown paper bag were the order of most days. After the divorce the change in Jemima was dramatic and even more so when her husband died a year later. For the first time in her life she was able to make her own decisions. She got a nice little job working in a charity shop with some lovely people who became good friends who would phone me if she had any problems. Jemima took over the household, doing the housework, washing and looking after Petie the cat. Every day she would walk the half mile to the town centre, order a cheese pastie (her favourite), and collect it after shopping on her way home. We would inevitably find her sitting asleep in her chair with the cat snuggled up on her knee.

Petie has been a godsend for us, giving love and company to Jemima. If she was unwell he would not leave her side and spent hours sleeping on her bed once she became bedridden.

We have never let her cook, not that she couldn't, but because she had spent the last 50 odd years cooking meals that her husband complained about or didn't eat. A thankless task we were not going to let happen ever again. She made a lovely cup of tea which was her way of welcoming us home.

I can't say it was easy having another woman in the house and we did clash, which I regret, but defend myself in as much that my emotional state during this time was, to say the least, erratic. Dealing with her husband, her family, my son, full time work, all took their toll. If only I had found those lovely anti-depressants sooner, I am sure I would have coped so much better.

Anyway that aside, the family agreed Jemima would spend 6 months in England with us and then 6 months abroad with her youngest son. Of course a year down the line we realised that this just wasn't going to happen as apparently it was not conducive to his lifestyle to have his Mother living with them. He actually said that! So she flew out every 2 years for 3 weeks to give us a break. Now she is unable to fly on her own she is with us full-time and I and D'Artagnan have become her full time carers as her dementia and old age take their toll.

Very little involvement from her youngest son, grand daughter or great-grandson over the years and now no interest or visits at all, just an annual visit by her youngest son. We are just thankful for Mother's dementia as at least she can't be hurt by this indifference!

I had thought I would include Jemima's dementia as part of this chapter, but it has become evident that this subject will need a chapter all of its' own. To see how this appalling disease takes hold please do have a read of my chapter on Living with Alzheimers.

Suffice it to say that Jemima has been living with us for the last 16 years and is now 96 years old.

During the time she has been with us I have aimed to give Jemima the freedom she craved. D'Artagnan and I endeavoured to take Jemima to the places she wanted to visit including a week in her home town up North. She also flew a helicopter for her 85th birthday! She wanted to do a dual parachute jump but I was unable to find anyone willing to take on the insurance for it. She has also been making an annual 2 week visit to Scotland to stay with her Sister-in-Law, happy in the knowledge that she could enjoy the stay without incessant phone calls from her husband.

The best thing for her, I believe, is the freedom she has had to come and go where and when she pleases without having a third degree on her return.

Whether I really agreed with the need for her to divorce him and not try the counselling, I can honestly say it has been a pleasure to see her grow in confidence and see her happy.

Making the decision to have Jemima live with us was made believing that the family would assist us, which didn't happen. Jemima's choice to live in her own little flat didn't pan out as by the time the divorce had gone through she just wanted to stay with us. We just hadn't put enough thought into how Jemima's ageing was going to progress and this has changed our lives so completely.

I am not wholly sure that in this instance, the choice, although the right one, was not one we could have, in all reality, known just what the ultimate consequences to our lives would be.

GRANDCHILDREN

M y two grand children are so very different and our relationship is as diverse as you can imagine!

Marie, my son (Ian's) daughter, is now in her late twenties and is a smart and beautiful girl. I bow to her Mother's ability to bring up such a well adjusted young lady, especially as she was a single mother. This constantly reminds me of my own failures.

Ian's relationship with the Mother of his child ended as expected due to his drug taking. I was so pleased when asked to continue being her GrandMother. So many breakups leave the grandparents in limbo and the families separated, so I was very lucky. Marie and I have been very close throughout her life and her many achievements make me so very proud. So very different from her Dad's inability to accept life, thank goodness. She just goes to show that being raised in a single parent home has in no way held her back or stopped her realising her dreams.

After studying for a degree Marie decided to take a gap year and travel. The people skills learnt from the many months of enticing people into a club in Greece or mixing with many nationalities have held her in good stead.

So many good times watching her grow up, firstly visiting weekly and fortnightly to eventually extending the times as she started filling her life with other interests. I have an especially lovely photograph of her at about 4 years old sitting in a chair at her home talking to me on the phone. The time captured for posterity and it would have made a lovely ad campaign for BT (telephone supplier)!

Growing up has not been an easy for her as at about 14 years old her Mother was diagnosed with breast cancer and she spent many months listening to her being sick and in pain whilst undergoing chemotherapy. She coped remarkably well, although she did suffer with dreadful anxiety whenever she left the house to go to school. Understandable really as she just didn't want to go out and be faced with a possible trauma, opting to be part of her Mother's recovery, and her panic attacks gave her that time. Thankfully her Mother has been in remission and continues to be healthy.

Having her Dad leave her when she was about 3 years old, Marie, at 18 decided she wanted to see him. I must admit to not being too encouraging over the years as I knew he was no longer the Dad he was or that she would remember. We have often talked about the reasons as I am very much a believer that in difficult situations you have to be very aware of why you are wanting to do something and ultimately who will benefit by it. Opening a door can often be difficult to close so you need to be sure of your motives and the effect on your future. So far she has visited him 3 times, and thankfully not got too involved.

In her late twenties now I am so very proud of her, her achievements, and the way she has dealt with issues that would have defeated lesser mortals.

I don't really know my Grandson, although it was not for want of trying to get to know him. Unfortunately at the time he was born, both D'Artagnan and I were very busy working full time and out most evenings and weekends either rehearsing or out playing with the band.

We had warned Lisa at the time she told us of her pregnancy that we were not able to be normal grandparents but that we would be happy to do our bit, she only had to ask. Unfortunately this just didn't happen as Lisa decided instead of giving us the opportunity to see Anthony she would never ask us and other than the odd time she called round for her 5 minute visit, Anthony felt uncomfortable and eventually refused to come over at all.

Perhaps not the best grandparents in the world, but he did have 2 other sets whose lives enabled them to fulfil that doting role. We did our bit Birthdays and Christmas, visiting and ultimately giving Anthony anything he wanted, such as a bicycle and later on a motorbike. Not once did he come round and visit, although I did ask him to let us see him on his bike when he was passing.

I don't think there was ever a time that we were not supportive of either Lisa or Anthony albeit within the constraints our lifestyle allowed.

Marie was very different accepting the limitations of our relationship and proved it when she was about 5 years old coming back from the library with a book called "My granddad is a rock star"!

I did tackle Lisa as often as I could regarding lack of access to Anthony, however, her answer was that it was not her job to tell us where and what he was up to, I should ring her. Her 3 week notice for us to see Anthony scuppered any chance we had of building any relationship especially as the first time I tried to book him she told me it would be 12 weeks before he was free!

Admittedly I understood this as Lisa's idea of bringing up Anthony was to return to work as soon as possible and put him with childminders and grandparents and then as he grew up, into after school clubs, football, basketball etc including Summer schools. He spent most free weekends with his grandparents on his Father's side.

I tried texting Anthony weekly, with no response or acknowledgement, so firstly I checked with him that I had the right mobile number and whether he was receiving my texts. Yes to both, and you would think that maybe our conversation would prompt him to participate, but no.

I take full responsibility for the lack of contact, at least from my side, as I should have tried harder, visited more often, been more involved in his life. Somewhere along the years I gave up as rebuff after rebuff takes it out of you.

Not so much a choice but resignation that my life was just too busy to continue a fight with my step-daughter, when all it would take was for her to be less intransigent, and be more willing so we could arrange some sort of meaningful access.

DOMESTIC VIOLENCE & ABUSE

S o much of the violence and abuse that takes place either within the family or outside of it can affect anyone. Throughout my life I have seen so much worse and sometimes some unbelievable abuse that can be perpetrated on one human being by another. These are just my experiences and how I managed to overcome or live with them.

Life changed dramatically for us all when Mum married my step father, Norman, a likeable, jolly Scotsman, who drove a train and unfortunately drank to excess. In a social environment he was the life and soul of the party and our evenings changed to going to pubs, clubs and hotels, sleeping in the car while Mum waited, sober, to get us all home safe.

Once in the car and at home he changed to a violent drunk, regularly throwing food and furniture and eventually beating Mum on what seemed like a nightly occurrence. Eventually, Mum took to getting us out of bed in the middle of the night, when we would push the car half a mile up the road and then drive to the fort and sleep in the car, returning only when Norman had left for work.

Mum had changed jobs and was now working for the District Commissioner at the fort and it was he that eventually became our saviour.

I vaguely remember incidents with Norman when I would lie on his bed with him, being cuddled and touched. To a small girl this was just a way of showing love for me and I saw nothing wrong with it. Little did I know that this was to be a warning for us all.

For the next 5 years my life seemed to be a mix of happiness and fear, until that dreadful night when he tried to kill Mum, beating her senseless and strangling her. How she got out the house I have no idea, but our Saviour rescued us all and before we knew it we were on a ship to England to join my Aunt and start a new life. I hated the day we boarded the train, with the Commissioner guarding us, and Norman trying to drag Mum out through the window!

Unfortunately this didn't mean, as we had thought, a Norman free zone, as it was only a couple of years later that he followed us to England and Mum took him back to try again. They bought a grocer shop to work together and this partnership lasted about 3 months before he was back down the pub. Back to the nights of rows, screams, fear and ineffectual visits from the Police.

By this time Caroline was approaching puberty and unfortunately got caught up in the violence, being constantly threatened with sexual violence if Mum was not willing at anytime to succumb to his drunken advances.

The final event happened when Mum was cooking dinner for Norman and the inevitable row started which culminated in Mum throwing a hot frying pan at him and we all left the house with minimum possessions that night.

Our choices were limited, with three children, a dog, and very little money. So we took a bus to the City and initially stayed above a café in a small B&B room which we all shared. Mum made friends with a salesman who regularly gave us free sausages and bacon to help us. It was nice to think someone wanted to help her with no ulterior motive. I can remember my Mum being horrified when she had managed to get a one room flat only to find that the building was tenanted by prostitutes, who much to her surprise became our protectors and chief babysitters when needed. Mum got a job and we continued travelling to school in our home town.

I have always wondered at the complete stupidity of the Social Services. Mum had got a job but needed another £20 to get through the week to cope with the added bus fares we needed and lunch money as we didn't have time to travel home and back again. She explained her difficulties and their answer was to tell her to reduce her hours from 40 a week to 11 a week and they would pay her £120 to top up her lack of earnings. Where is the logic in that? I don't think Mum ever took up the offer as she was of the old school where you worked if you could. However it did mean that we had to cut down considerably. I remember every Saturday Mum would buy a huge bar of chocolate that we shared, any other chocolates we had to buy with our pocket money! Later on mine of course went on cigarettes! Martin supplemented his income by raiding Mum's cash boxes which she studiously filled each week with the money needed to pay the bills.

We moved around a lot during those 'hiding' years but Mum never made us feel that we were lacking in any way.

Mum took the step to start divorce proceedings. A hard time for my brother who was the chief witness in court. He tried hard to cope with his role as man of the house but his past inability to protect the family led to him running away at the age of 16 to join the Merchant Navy which broke all our hearts and especially Mum who could never come to terms with the criminal he became over the years. The only time he visited was when he wanted money which after a while became a wedge between them that never eased.

The last I heard from my Step-Dad was that he had moved to Scotland and married a woman who could drink him under the table, so a match made in hell! Where is he now? I care less and have never wanted to see him again.

This wasn't to be my last experience of domestic violence. My sister married young and had 2 lovely children, both who remain close. Unfortunately her husband found the responsibility just too much and resorted to 4 years of brutality which my sister has never come to terms with. Like me she has never been willing to undertake counselling and open those 'closed' doors once again. Although, I did eventually go to counselling I fully understood her reluctance.

I was not really aware of Caroline's marital problems until they came to live with my Mum and me. Ian was about 3 months old then. Half way through breast feeding I heard screaming and shouting, and found my sister being dragged by her hair up the corridor, with Mum trying to intervene. He attacked Mum and had her on the floor with his hands round her neck at which time I ran for the door to get help. Running down the road in a nightie, covered in black paint, (Mum had thrown a pot of black paint at him which covered us all), being pursued by HIM, I managed to get one of our neighbours to open the door.

What made me laugh, although not at the time, was that Caroline's husband had decided to hold Mum, Caroline and her 2 children and of course Ian hostage with a shotgun. When the policeman arrived (one bobby on a bike) and I told him again about the gun, we then had to wait for nearly an hour while the Police Commissioner arrived with 2 ambulances, a fire engine, a dog handler and 4 police cars. Then we all waited for another 45 minutes while a bullet proof vest was found before anything was done about resolving the situation.

Meantime I was left in my neighbours house wondering what was happening at home and whether anyone was still alive! As it was he handed the shotgun out the window and went to work and the police let him! The police doctor came and declared that Caroline's husband definitely had a problem. However, he managed to convince said Doctor that living with 3 women was his problem and I think the Doctor agreed with him and no further action was taken to curb his aggressive and mindless violent nature!

24 hour police protection and injunctions were ineffective as every time he came round my sister was coerced into seeing him by the police. At one time he started dragging her into his car while the police watched! They say times have changed, but I am not so sure they have.

I have always tried to support any of my friends or family who need 'someone' to be in their corner and help them to do whatever it takes, as is attested to by the fact that my Mum-in-Law escaped from her 56 year abusive relationship at the age of 80 and has been living with us ever since.

The shame of it all was that my mother-in-law suffered mental and physical abuse for those 56 years without really knowing what it was, but that is her story, not mine, to tell. Suffice to say that although physical abuse was few and far between, the controlling and jealous behaviour was abuse in a different way. She only had money when he gave it to her, and then she would have to account for every penny, bringing the change and receipts home for him to check. He would also give her £20 a week for doing the housework, but again she would need to account for her spending. Her opinions didn't count and he always shouted her down so in the end she decided it was better not to speak, which in turn annoyed him! She couldn't win.

I suppose the reason she put up with it for so long was that this was normal behaviour for her time, when men looked on women as chattels or possessions. This was attested during the divorce hearing when he told the judge that "His wife had been removed from his home without his consent"! The look on the judge's face said it all. Even when she told him that his wife didn't need his consent to do anything, he would not accept it. The thing that stands out throughout all of this is that there are an awful lot of older women (and men) who suffer this type of abuse because most women at that time had been told by their Mothers that they should obey their husband, just as she had in her own time.

At the time I never understood why my Mum kept taking my step dad back, was it fear of the unknown having to bring up 3 children alone, maybe fear of him by not taking him back, or maybe she just convinced herself that she loved him. Whatever the reason her decisions definitely affected us children in one way or another and in different ways determined our futures.

Caroline never trusting in an intimate relationship ever again, Martin who went off the rails and has struggled over the years to settle down, and me, well I will leave you to draw your own conclusions from my story.

Although these experiences were mine just because I was there, I learnt a valuable lesson that carried me through all my relationships. Any one who has shown even the inkling of violence towards me or mine are out the door pronto and no second chances!

All I can say really say about these abusive relationships is that they all go away in the end and all you need is the right support at the right time! There is so much more out there now than there ever was in my Mum or Sister's day.

Abuse sits well within the realms of domestic violence but also outside of it.

I was raped when I was 20 years old. I had been working at a nightclub 6 nights a week and my son was just 2 years old. The man concerned was a regular that never hit on me or bought me a drink. Always just chatting and sociable and had been coming to the club every week for about 2 years. One night he couldn't get a taxi and I offered to give him a lift home which he gratefully accepted. We chatted as we drove for about 3 miles when he directed me up a dark lane and asked me to stop as he would walk from there. Suddenly he was all over me, ripping my clothes and hitting me as I tried to fight back. I gave in and let him have his way, which he did and then promptly got out of the car and said thanks for the lift. I sat there crying for almost an hour, locking the car doors just in case he came back and then drove home. I was living with Mum at the time so I crept in, it was by then 3am, and she was asleep. I showered and threw away my clothes, crying quietly all the time. I didn't tell anyone for many years. The following week I was dreading going to work but he appeared as usual and acted like nothing had happened.

I did think about going to the Police to report him, but the more I thought about it I realised that no-one would believe me. I had willingly given him a lift, I had washed and thrown any evidence away and there was that nagging feeling that it would end up with me being put on trial. After all I was a single parent with one abortion behind me, working at a nightclub and had had several sexual relationships since I was 17.

He did eventually get banged up after raping several young girls and I do feel guilty that maybe if I had drawn attention to my rape these girls would have been saved what could be for them a life changing event. For me I decided to learn from this experience and never put myself in that position again. It would not affect the rest of my life, I wouldn't let him have the satisfaction!

Although I loved my job at the Nightclub I did have to put up with constant abuse by my Manager for about 2 years. As I was always the last one cashing up or cleaning the kitchen I would often find that he had chivvied everyone out of the club and locked the door. He insisted we had a downtime drink before he would pay me my wages. This slowly progressed to him grabbing hold of me and chasing me round the club trying to get his wicked way with me, even to the extent of pinning me down on the dance floor. I am proud of myself that throughout these 2 years, persistent as he was, I never gave in. It was only when he started to call round at my flat at 3am that I eventually told him where to go. By then, if I lost my job, then I lost my job! Up until then I was too reliant on the job to make any waves.

Another event occurred when I was 17 when I was staying with a friend. It was all OK to start with but then her husband started catching me alone attempting to kiss and touch me. I didn't want to upset my friend so just started avoiding him at every possible turn, ensuring I was not caught in my dressing gown but fully dressed, as fighting him off was a little easier. Worse was to come when I woke up from sleep one night to find someone touching my breasts and running hands up and down my body. I realised who it was and was so embarrassed and unsure how to react that I stirred, made some noises and he eventually went away. However, these nightly visits became more regular and I realised that this was not going to stop. How was I to stop it? I couldn't ask for a lock on my bedroom door without having to tell my friend why. In the end I sat up in bed as he started to touch me one night and in no uncertain terms told him to stop this or I would tell his wife. This stopped him in his tracks and I only wish I had had the courage to stand up to him sooner. Needless to say I didn't stay long with my friend.

The question of whether I should have told my friend is one that has bugged me throughout the years. At the time I felt so violated, ashamed and guilty, as if it was my fault that her husband was behaving this way, and this is a secret I have kept through the years until sharing now with you. If I had been older and less vulnerable, maybe things would have been very different and I would not have had to put up with all that trauma, when I was just going into my own trauma of expecting a baby and becoming a single mother.

From my experience if someone is violent or abusive towards you it will only get worse unless the person gets treatment. Meeting up with so many people during the years who have suffered I realise that my experiences are minimal compared with some of the atrocities that women and men suffer at the hands of their partners. Getting out is not easy, but there is so much more help available now, that if you can take that first step things can only improve. Most perpetrators eventually give up and disappear from your life, whether it is to prison or finding someone more willing to put up with this kind of treatment. Don't keep quiet, get help, and protect your family and yourself from these kind of people.

Perpetrators of violence and abuse are very clever people, convincing their loved ones it was a one off (each time), professing undying love and generally keeping that level of control over you. They convince you that each incident is your fault and in the end you believe them. No-one has the right to control another human being by fear and/or intimidation. Be strong and believe in yourself, it is rarely you that is at fault.

HEALTH

O verall I suppose I have been very lucky with my health, although have gone through some very traumatic experiences. We all wonder how we will cope when given bad news or told we need an operation. So much depends on what is happening in your life at the time.

Starting at the beginning I had all the usual childhood illnesses, in fact my Mother always insisted on taking us out of school to mix with neighbours children so that we could catch whatever it was going round at the time. Certainly the schools in Africa were very receptive to this idea and all the families tended to do this. So being ill when we were young, once over the worst of it, be it mumps or chicken pox, we would have lots of fun being quarantined together. No doubt a headache for the Mum of the moment!

We used to play chase through the maize fields, tying the plants to form arches which we then ran through. Unfortunately I managed to fall over straight onto a piece of glass and cut my knee open. It was about an inch in length and about half an inch deep and didn't bleed straight away so I didn't really notice it. Once the bleeding started, I started crying and we all went home. Mum held the two sides together and put tape on it. 10 minutes later we were out in the field again! Those were the days when Health and Safety and Accident & Emergency just didn't exist!

I can't remember much else happening to me even when we got to England. Oh yes, I did manage to break a tiny bone in my foot when I went to my middle school. I was racing out of the canteen when I slipped and my foot swelled up very quickly. The reason I really remember this is that when I got to hospital the Doctor bent my foot almost in half, asking me if that hurt! Just to add to that he then proceeded to put the biggest needle into the side of my foot and wiggle it around for good measure!

Early teens just the usual problems with periods and getting a birth pill that worked. Too late of course for me as I managed to get pregnant a second time when my son was just 3 years old. This time I took the step of having an abortion. Too young to really appreciate the guilt and regrets I would have in my later years but when you are a single parent struggling with one child the enormity of having another is just overwhelming. I think often of the little girl I gave up on and the guilt I felt at the time. I woke up crying from the operation and didn't stop for the rest of the day.

Returning from a holiday in Italy in my early twenties I came home covered in a rash, and I mean covered. All over my face, neck, arms, chest, but not my legs. The first consultant decided I was allergic to the sun, but the creams and potions didn't make any difference. He was perturbed when the rash continued all through the winter. Not that he had a rational answer for that when asked, so I just stopped going. Some 3 years later the second consultant decided that I had eczema so another set of creams and potions which again didn't work. He was baffled because my rash didn't itch! Some 5 years later the third consultant decided I had some sort of acne but was baffled by the fact that the rash never erupted. Different creams and potions that again didn't work. By this time the rash was coming and going and had at last stopped appearing on my face. Something that made my life at least bearable having stopped looking into the mirror whilst plastering loads of make up to try and cover it up. Of course throughout this time I couldn't go swimming down the beach and my wardrobe consisted of high necked, sleeved tops!

The final consultant some 5 years later did a biopsy and decided I had some kind of lupus, but again the creams and potions didn't work. So as a last resort he decided to give me some cancer pills, which he informed me would mean that my body would be too used to them should I contract cancer at a later stage. On reading the gumph in the box it also transpired that these pills could make me go permanently blind. Although seeing the funny side of his thinking that if the rash didn't go at least I wouldn't be able to see it, I decided not to go down that route and gave up on pursuing this any further.

To this day I still have a rash on the tops of my arms and chest which appears and disappears for no good reason and I guess after all the experiences I have been through I just have to put up with it. Luckily for me after all these years D'Artagnan doesn't see the rash as he sees the real me and not just the spotty, stretch marked, slightly wobbly body of today. Amazingly D'Artagnan started growing Aloe Vera plants and at his insistence I rubbed the sap on the rash and for the first time in my life I am going to a wedding wearing a lovely low necked, sleeveless silk top. Shame about the wrinkles and bat wings!

In my late twenties I found a lump on the side of my right breast and went to see a consultant. It was a very nerve racking time waiting for the appointment but shocking when I actually got there. I don't know if anyone else has encountered this but after sticking a needle into my boob the consultant proceeded to feel my breasts and then I noticed he was actually rubbing himself up and down my knees as I sat on the bed! Too young, too naïve and too embarrassed to say anything I left. An operation was arranged for the following week in a private hospital and the lump was removed. I then waited a further 3 weeks before hearing any more about it. So again a very worrying time, to be dispelled when told it was benign.

I suppose I remained healthy for the next 10 years as life looking after my son, getting married and having a step- daughter sort of took over.

D'Artagnan and I had often talked about whether to have another child or not, but neither of us were very keen, so we took the decision for me to be sterilised and get a dog instead! We are amazed that at the time I was not allowed to make that decision without his consent as it was such a final step and irreversible. So imagine our surprise when in my forties I became pregnant!

In fact it was such a surprise that it never entered our heads when I became racked with pain. For nearly 3 months I saw 6 doctors and was treated for all manner of things. Each one different. I was still working full-time and remember the day I had a really excruciating pain that I immediately took myself off to casualty. This was about 1pm. A young junior doctor gave me one of those oh so intimate examinations (I think she tried to stick her whole hand up there)! She decided it was possibly cysts and suggested she would make an outpatients appointment for me.

By this time (5pm) I felt I was dying with the pain and feeling worse and worse. Making a fuss about getting some pethidine to ease the pain she arranged for me to go to another hospital to have the medicine administered. So I rang my son to come and drive the car for me. We stopped for petrol and drove the 10 miles. Once in the hospital I was put in bed, and sent my son home with the car to let D'Artagnan know what was happening. These were the days before the general proliferation of mobile phones. Immediately I had a blood test and an hour later when he arrived we were told that I was pregnant. Unfortunately for me it was ectopic, (the foetus was in the fallopian tube), it had burst and I was in surgery by 7pm. In fact the surgeon came up the next morning to tell me how lucky I had been as they had taken a copious amount of blood out of me and if I had gone home, as the junior doctor suggested, I would have been dead before the morning. A good decision to stand up to authority! Over the following year the lack of hormones made living with me worse than it had ever been. Trying to prove to the Doctors that I couldn't control my moods, felt tired and to some extent suicidal, led to more tests when he agreed that my remaining ovary was not working and arranged for a consultant appointment to discuss the next step.

Their decision, a year later, was that I had a hysterectomy and my remaining fallopian tube and ovary removed. I was put on hormone replacement therapy and have been on that ever since. What a boon that is! No more periods, no more emotional ups and downs, and I even look younger than my current years, or so I am told. Speaking to the hospital regarding the previous sterilisation, suddenly it was not 100%, as I said, evidently not!

As you can imagine depression has been ever present throughout my adult life, most of the time undiagnosed. It only became diagnosed when I had trouble at my last job, which you can read about in my career and workplace bullying chapters. To cope during these depressions I would go and re-invent myself. I changed my hair colour and style and updated my clothes to match the new me. This did help me get through a lot during those years.

I suppose depression comes in varying degrees and up until 3 years ago I had always managed it with the help of D'Artagnan and my family. Suddenly I was standing on railway platforms thinking about how quick it would be if I just stepped forward. I took myself to the Doctor when I found myself not just thinking about it but actually moving closer to the edge! Anti-depressants did the job and continue to keep me on a level. Mind you D'Artagnan has always said that I am not me on these pills, but after all this time I am not sure who I was that is so different from today. I think of it as a blessing that I no longer have hysteria, paranoia, depression, mood swings or want to throw myself under a train. Sounds good to me!

Counselling was interesting but resolved little, just a few sound bites and in the end I just agreed with whatever she felt she had achieved. I had avoided counselling for many years as I could not see the benefit of opening doors that I had closed, albeit, without resolving any of the issues. However, I had learnt to live with them! I must admit, the close encounters with National Rail, made me agree to see a counsellor. Initially it was everything I thought it would be, me crying a lot, talking in between when possible, and sitting opposite someone with absolutely no solutions or strategies to offer. After 8 sessions, all I seemed to be doing was bringing all those long suppressed issues back to the surface. I suppose she thought that if I thought about all the old issues, I might be able to stop thinking about the latest issues. Her most consistent comment each session was "Do you feel like a victim?" or "There you are, Victim!". As I told her each time she stated it, I have never felt a victim of anything but circumstance, the choices available and the decisions I chose to make. Whatever her reasoning, I felt little benefit, other than being able to blub like a baby without upsetting the family around me. I decided that locking the bathroom door, putting on the radio and crying my heart out was a cheaper option and one that was definitely less hurtful to me!

Just to complete my catalogue of health problems my breasts recently started excreting fluid. I knew for sure I wasn't pregnant, nothing left you see! Again the worries and stress returned and D'Artagnan came with me to my first appointment at the breast clinic. An examination and a chat and then sent away for a week while they reviewed the results. Luckily for me they decided it was just the ducts in the breast and that the fluid was benign. I had a choice of putting up with it or having an operation to remove the ducts. I decided to put up with it. That is until recently when pus suddenly appeared from one of the ducts. Still the consultant did say only to worry if they started bleeding, so I just give them a squeeze regularly and although the clear fluid is still there the pus seems to have stopped. Well there's not so much of it.

I really can't face up to having more surgery unless there really is no option, and even then I would think twice about it. Having seen so many of my friends going through cancer and the results of operations, chemo therapy, radiation etc and then die a horrible death, I don't think I could be brave enough to follow their example.

For many years I taught Yoga to a select group of friends, tailored to meet their needs as they were all over 50 when I first started with them. My body felt great, however, giving it up as my latest job was sending me away a lot and with Jemima to look after, I discovered an interesting bit of information.

My back has always given me trouble but it has always been manageable with pain killers. I put this down to the many years in catering lifting heavy crates and bending over tables, so was really expecting it. What I wasn't expecting was when the Consultant at the hospital said my Yoga had stretched the muscles in my back to the extent that they were no longer holding my spine in place, hence the odd disc jumping out! Yoga is still not on due to Jemima mainly, but no doubt a bit of it is my apathy when I have eventually put her to bed after a fractious day!

I suppose one of the most devastating things that could happen to anyone, is losing your teeth. Over the years I had lost a couple of teeth due to some of my second teeth lodging themselves in my gums and because of this I only had the choice of wearing a denture. Over the years I lost more and more and eventually have ended up with a full set of top dentures.

This happened during my last years in training for the software company, so you can imagine how I felt. One week I had teeth and the next I had a full denture! My first training session was full of spit and whistles. The class found it immensely funny when I apologised in advance that I was breaking in a new set of teeth for a friend! With the help of glue and a lot of perseverance I only spit and whistle occasionally!

There have been some advantages although it took me a while of depression about the whole situation before realising that the dentist had done me a favour. No longer were my teeth crooked, stained and with gaps, suddenly I had the most gorgeous smile, at least I thought so. However the dentist had done such a good job that most people didn't realise what had changed in me, but that whatever it was, it was an improvement.

Add to that the vanity of having cosmetic surgery on my top eyelids, which were quite hooded, and suddenly at the age of 50+, with new teeth and wide open eyes, I was happy with my appearance at last! As D'Artagnan has always told me, I am like a bottle of fine wine, much improved with age. I do remind him occasionally that all bottles of wine go sour in the end.

The question now is do I have more cosmetic surgery to get rid of my increasing wrinkles and double chin, continue to fight age, or just give in? Maybe this will be my next adventure?

BETRAYAL

Betrayal comes in many guises and in my experience these are usually brought about by our own expectations of what constitutes friendship.

The first time was when I was 16 and going out with who I now realise after all these years, 'a bit of rough', 'a misogynist', 'a philanderer', and 'self centred pig'! Of course at that age I thought he was the love of my life and the best thing to have ever happened to me. How wrong can one be. Anyway I digress, as the story is really about my best friend for 6 years, Paula, having attended the same school and spent all our time together from the age of 11. She being the pretty, petite one and me being the fat, frumpy one. But she never made me feel like that and I loved our close relationship.

We spent most school lunchtimes in the local rest garden smoking the 5 Cadet cigarettes purchased with our pooled 'dinner' money. We lived in each other's pockets for the whole of our relationship. Experimenting with make up and clothes, getting into trouble at school, going everywhere together and even teaming up with boys who were best friends just so we could keep together.

Several times we told our parents that we were staying at each other's houses just so we could stay out later, and ended up sleeping rough. Boy that was cold and frightening!

This was to all change when I discovered that she had been having an affair behind my back with the love of my life. Of course I blamed her when really I should have realised that she was as flattered as I was that he was interested. Be that as it may she still went behind my back and I never forgave her for it. She moved away to the West Country and my relationship with 'the pig' continued until he asked me to marry him then dumped me, then asked me again, and then dumped me yet again and got married to someone else. All within the space of 3 weeks!

I did receive a telephone call from Paula some 18 months later asking me to help her re-locate back to the area and I am ashamed to say that I told her I never wanted to see her again and why did she think I would want her back in my life.

I often wonder to this day where she is and how she is doing and often search through social media hoping to see her picture as I know she got married, had a child and of course changed her name. I am still unsure that if I did find her again whether I would trust her with me and mine!

My next encounter with betrayal was by my next best friend and work colleague. At the time it was bruising and hurtful. I had worked with this lady for some 10 years and found myself sacked 2 nights before Christmas.

I first met Jane when I was 15 as she owned a Restaurant that opened as a coffee bar in the evenings. This was the only place, other than a pub, where the local youth could go and meet. She was the most beautiful woman I had ever seen, matching my idol since I was 11 years old, Doris Day. Over the years I found that not only was she beautiful on the outside but she was beautiful on the inside.

Parents were happy to know their children/teens were in a safe place and were kept on the straight and narrow. No feet on chairs, no gum under the tables, no arguments, just a fun place to meet up. No alcohol but a juke box playing the latest sounds. Dances were held with a live band when a social event called for it.

My generation had the mods and rockers every evening in the same place, chatting and playing the football table out in the back room. The front parking area had as many scooters as it did motorbikes. My attire always depended on who I was going out with at the time, either a parka or a leather jacket. Outside of the coffee bar the usual tricks were played between the two opposing sides and I was happy to join in pinching the flags flying off scooters or jeering at the leather clad greasers!

The local police dropped in for coffee between shifts and got on well with us all. Such a shame this generation can't appreciate the same familiarity we had with their local constabulary. I remember beating quite a few of the boys in blue on the football table. Then there was one fireworks night when a couple of the police popped in for coffee and decided to help us set off the fireworks for the kids. Within minutes they had managed to set the whole box alight! Best fireworks night ever, as rockets, catherine wheels, bangers etc completely filled the back yard, bouncing of the walls and shooting into the sky. By then we were all inside, watching the display through the windows, but I can honestly say that was the most spectacular 10 minutes ever. That will teach the local cops that just maybe we didn't need to be kept safe by them after all. Maybe we would have done better ourselves. The children decided they wanted that to happen every year and could we invite more of their friends to watch it.

Jane also became the Manager of a local football team that she put together and all in all they did very well in the local league. I remember the Saturday afternoons spent in the field watching them play and dispensing oranges at half time.

Jane was and is to this day loved by and never forgotten by all the generations that were lucky enough to have grown up with her as a mentor and friend.

Anyway back to the point of my story, I started working on a Saturday as a waitress and thrived on her help and advice. After having my son I needed part-time work and as Jane had also had a son about the same age it seemed natural that I would work part-time through the week. We shared the caring of the boys when they were at the cot stage and throughout the next 9 years and became less like Mother and daughter and more like friends. She was very much instrumental in helping me to attain some confidence in myself and my abilities.

Over those years we became closer and spent much of our time together sharing the extra work that goes with running a restaurant. I would go to the cash and carry, stay up throughout the night just before Christmas to assist with making hundreds of fresh mince pies and sausage rolls, and generally helping with whatever was needed. In return Jane would often lend me her car to go home and return the following morning, which made my life so much easier at that time.

I felt a very close bond with Jane that was cemented when her marriage broke up and she was taken ill. Firstly I took her to my home with her youngest son and kept her safe while she sorted out getting her husband out of the restaurant and her back in. My son and I moved in with her and I slept fully clothed each night so that should her violent husband break in I could get out the window to get the Police. Then I helped her keep the restaurant open and she taught me to cook and manage the restaurant while she was incapacitated. She was such a good teacher that unless anyone came into the kitchen they would never have known whether it was me or her working that day. However, the one thing I never could master was her knack of making the most beautiful pastries, so the customers had to do without for the 6 weeks before Jane was well enough to take over again. For the next few years I would say we were quite inseparable, at least that was the way it felt to me.

Things changed when she remarried, as it should have, and I was so happy that she had found someone that she could share her life with. I must admit though to feeling somewhat sad that when she got married I was not invited to the wedding as 'it was family only' and when asked if I would open the restaurant that day and prepare the wedding dinner for their return, I was happy to do so. A few days before the wedding took place I found out that other people were attending that in my eyes were not 'family', so must admit to feeling resentful and I regret to say that my behaviour must have been hurtful to her as I was very churlish when she came back and gave me her bouquet. Even more so when I phoned her the night before to say I was ill and she said don't worry I will close the restaurant! Needless to say I got over my feelings and opened the restaurant and cooked and served the meal. I was not invited to join the party!

Anyway over the next few months her new husband, who I considered a friend, started being very rude to me. Accusing me of trying to force my way in to her business. I could no longer 'borrow' the car, or help with the cash and carry. I never did really understand what happened but believe she was put in the position of making a choice, me or him? It took me a long time to realise that if the shoe was on the other foot I would have done the same.

I do remember that night so vividly. D'Artagnan was going out for a boy's night out and was upstairs getting ready. When Jane left, I was crying hysterically in the kitchen, on my hands and knees scrubbing the floor. It was a way of channelling my anger and sadness at the events taking place. What was I going to do now? Not only had I lost my job but also my best friend!

This supposed betrayal did have a silver lining as I had to re-look at my life and where I was going. On reflection this was the catalyst to the rest of my life. I re-trained, changed my career and ultimately my life. I learned a lot about myself and the possibilities that are out there if you just have the courage. D'Artagnan was of course there beside and behind me giving me the confidence to forge ahead.

One thing I have learnt as the years passed is that betrayal is not always what it appears to be and only seeing it from one side can make you bitter, resentful and can also lead you to believe that the fault lies with you. When in fact if you do what I did you can go out there and find a stronger you in the process.

Jane and I are firm friends now having the good fortune to meet up some years later and clear the air. Life is just too short to lose good friends so it is worth biding your time and waiting until the opportunity presents itself to rectify a relationship. I am so glad that we managed to do that. I owe her such a lot and feel I can never repay the debt for her friendship and guidance during those difficult years.

I have always seen myself as a good friend, always there when needed, do anything I can to help in the bad times, and fun to be within the good times. However, with writing this book I have realised that other than Jane, I have never managed to hold on to those I thought of as 'good' friends.

I met a girl once who had two little girls and her marriage had just failed. She was distraught and I spent as much time as work allowed visiting her on my day's off and taking her out. I even managed to find her a part-time job to fit in with school hours. Our friendship continued until she met another man, at which stage she was less available. She never rang me and put me off when I called. It was some years later that I bumped into her and was well and truly ticked off for 'dumping' her!

Most of my friendships have been brought about by their need for me during trying times, and without fail, all of these friendships disappear once they are sorted.

As I see contact drifting off from their end I try to keep in touch and give up when I don't get a response. The hurt of not knowing why is the hardest thing to get over. Constantly asking myself what did I do wrong? Even picking up contact again after many years apart, I find that I just can't get that friendship back.

You will no doubt find yourself, as I do, coming up with all the reasons why, such as, 'Their lives have changed' or 'They don't live so close now' or 'They don't have the time'. None of which really answer the question for you. After all, you will travel the distance to visit, you find the time to keep in touch, you will drop everything to be there for them.

I have come to the conclusion that it does not pay to get too involved in your friends personal lives as keeping you as a friend just reminds them of their own failures or bad times.

WORK, AMBITION AND CAREER

School had done little to get me to the top of the class or to have any idea on what I would want to do when I left to go out in the adult world. Oh how envious I was watching my school friends follow their ambitions and become the person they set their heart on since childhood. Guided by my Mum I took typing and shorthand lessons as this, she said, would always give me work in so many different fields. She had been a secretary most of her later working life.

Glad to be out of school I got a job in a small building society and became secretary to the Secretary (never could work that one out). Proof at once that Mum's advice had started me on a career path.

Over the years I have had many varied jobs and returned to undertake training on more than one occasion in order to progress. I must admit to hating the factory mentality so as soon as a job became mundane, or I could do it, I moved on to something new.

There is of course the element of being made redundant, to which I must confess has happened to me more than once! But I truly believe that these helped shape my working life. Forcing me to make a move, most times, when I was ready for it, but not yet had the courage to go back into the job market. Getting older does have a major effect on whether you can move on, and perhaps why I stayed in my last formal job for longer than I really wanted.

Getting over the initial shock at redundancy and anger at not being wanted, followed by the inevitable recriminations of I should have said this, or I should have said that, leading to grief and eventual lack of self worth. All of which have absolutely no effect on the outcome of the event and somehow manage to disrupt your home life and turn it upside down.

The first time was the worst, but I eventually picked myself up, re-trained and went into a new type of work. I would like to mention here that it was D'Artagnan who saved me. By 6 months he really just couldn't cope with my mood swings, outbursts, tears, etc. and threatened to leave me! So thank you so much my lovely man as you are always saving me from myself.

The second and third time got even easier, re-training and changing, not only my job but myself.

Just to give you some idea of my career, here they are in order.

Greengrocer assistant (age 14) A Saturday job giving me the money to pay for make up etc and supplemented my pocket money. I hated having to cook the beetroot and serve it, made my fingers purple, but the kit kat with a cup of tea made up for it and to this day that is my favourite combination. This was just the start of my people skills that would take me through the rest of my working career.

Secretary/PA at a Building Society - My first real job from leaving school. It was here that I realised my shorthand was iffy and my typing speeds and accuracy left a lot to be desired, but over the next 18 months with a brilliant, patient boss my confidence started growing. Thank goodness the days of carbon copies and non-correctable type are at last over.

Unfortunately my career, such as it was, never got off the ground when I managed to get myself pregnant at 17 and a single mother at 18 years old. One good thing was that it was during this time that my Mum taught me to drive her old Morris Minor traveller, when I learnt to change tyres, clutch cables and how to crank a car to start in the cold, wet weather. I hasten to add that this car was all we could afford at the time. How cars have changed now to an unidentifiable mystery under the bonnet that requires a mechanic with an IT degree to mend it! At least our car would start on the iciest of mornings whilst other newer cars sat at the roadside draining their batteries.

Cleaner - this was once a week for a professional couple with a large private flat, with wooden floors, designer kitchen, windows from floor to ceiling and 2 very messy people. The good thing was that I could take Ian with me in his pram soon after he was born. About the only good thing about that job! Every week she would present me with additional things to do, like polish the wooden floors throughout the flat and wash the windows as well as the usual tasks and all in 2 hours. This was my first experience of being paid only for the hours agreed rather the actual hours required to do the job.

Taxi despatcher - this was a useful little job that enabled me to take Ian with me when he was at the 'in the carry cot' stage. Once he started crawling the job got a little more frantic and as soon as he stood up on those little chubby legs of his, I left.

Waitress/Cook - at our local cafe where we all used to congregate after school and in the evenings. I started working part-time to fit in with pre-school hours at my son's nursery and later on it became almost a full time job. The owner, Jane, was to become my most staunch and loyal friend and is still very much in my life now. Initially I just waitressed and found that working with people was fun. I was efficient and quick and able to know exactly where and what was needed by the customers during a busy lunchtime with over 40 covers. Something that seems to be missing in this latest generation. It is so frustrating to be served by someone who is not aware of where you are in the queue, doesn't actually listen to your order, and spends most of the time chatting to his/her colleagues or playing with their mobile phones.

Jane started an outside catering business with a friend of hers that she ran alongside the restaurant and it was natural that I joined her as waitress and dogs body. Going to the cash and carry, loading the cars/vans with equipment and food, transporting to the venue and racing back to the restaurant mid function to collect a missing item or two. To this day Jane and I laugh at how I would drive back to the restaurant sometimes some 20 miles away to collect the cake knife for the wedding cake. We both wonder why we never thought to just go over the road and buy one!

We had many a laugh and each function was enjoyable but hard graft. Loading, unloading, preparing, serving, clearing up, washing up, loading, unloading and finishing at 2or 3 o'clock in the morning. This after having worked in the restaurant until 3pm and then the function from 5pm. I would shoot home and settle Ian with a babysitter.

I remember going over to a function one day and I was following Jane who had a van load of apple crumbles laid in their containers over the back of the van. She had to brake violently because of some nut in front and opening the doors we found 24 trays all bunched up at the front with crumble everywhere. No time to do much but save as much as we could and instead of silver servicing from the trays we plated it up! Of course the simplest solution would have been to make up the fruit and the crumble separately and then assemble it at the venue.

Or the time we did a function for a room full of very drunk policemen who spent most of the evening putting their hands up my mini skirt and pinging my suspender belt. This was at the time when not many women were in the police force. Not much I could do about it as my hands were carrying a large, hot, silver tray and of course the spoon and fork. Come to think of it my tips were extremely generous from both the restaurant and the functions, thanks to that mini skirt!

Jane and I spent a lot of time together when not working, including the weekends taking the children out or painting the café, railings or table and chairs. One weekend, covered in paint we decided to go to the cinema, and not bothering to change or wash, off we went and watched the latest movie based on Cinderella. We sang along in the cinema and had a lovely break from all the painting. On the way back to the car we were talking about how in movies when someone starts singing, no one around takes any notice. To prove the point Jane and I proceeded to sing the songs and dance as we moved along the pavement, and it is quite true, most people ignored us or we got a look of bemusement at these 2 forty-something's just letting go. I can definitely recommend this exercise as it lifts the spirits and just makes you laugh. The painting got finished in record time as we continued singing and dancing in private!

There was the time Jane wanted to put a shed up in the back garden of the café so we could store things, and were reliably informed that we would need to build a base for it to sit on. So with a bit of advice on the correct sand to cement ratio and how to put up sidings, away we went, only to find that just about every male who came in to the café that day decided we needed advice. Much to their chagrin we explained that laying a base is just like baking a cake, first of all you mix the ingredients, prepare the tin and then fill it up and smooth it off, just like icing the cake. To this day the base is still as smooth and rock steady as it was the day we laid it.

Why is it that some men just don't think women can cope or carry out tasks once designated as the male domain. Maybe they feel usurped?

Although this job was hard work and the pay negligible working with my best friend was reward enough as we supported each other and knew that whatever happened we would be there for one another. Although we did have a blip in our relationship as you have already read about in my Betrayal chapter.

Nightclub Receptionist - Whilst working in the restaurant in the early years I also took on 6 nights at the local Nightclub as a receptionist. This was before the outside catering took over. This was an interesting time as I started there while carrying my son and continued for some years after he was born. Thank goodness for Mum who made this possible by babysitting for me.

The job suited me and I loved having to dress up and have a social life without having to get involved. Although I do remember that my alcohol intake was very high as everyone bought me drinks and after

12 whisky and dry gingers I would get in my car and drive the 15 miles home at 2am. I never did get stopped but then that was a different time when people took responsibility for themselves rather than have the government decide for us. Driving through river country also meant that more often than not I was driving at 4 miles an hour due to thick fog, so maybe that is why I was so lucky!

The nightclub was my first experience of sexual harassment at work by my boss and rape by a so called 'friend'. More on this in my chapter on Harassment and Bullying in the Workplace and Domestic Violence and Abuse.

PA to a Managing Director of a pharmaceutical company - I had retrained to brush up on my secretarial skills and landed what I thought was a dream job. Unfortunately I was to work for one of the most foul mouthed, arrogant and horrible men it has been my misfortune to work for. There were lots of issues with this job, other than the Boss. Every day I struggled with an electric typewriter that was so sensitive it just seemed to print whatever key I breathed on! Not easy when once a month I would have to type his accounts onto an A3 spreadsheet with 13 copies in the typewriter. One mistake and it took ages to insert bits of paper between the copies and then carefully rub out the offending text, then trying to line it up again, only to find he rejected the final version and made me do it again. Taking shorthand down of unfamiliar pharmaceutical jargon was a nightmare. Needless to say I lasted only 6 months but managed to delete his wages software on my last day! He deserved it even if I didn't do it on purpose. Those of you who use a computer know what I mean when you are presented with a Yes/No option - I evidently chose the wrong one. So fire me, oh too late, I resigned! Again more of this in my Workplace Harassment and Bullying chapter.

Secretary at a large corporate company - worked for one man with a department of some 250 mostly men. I don't know why, but I have always enjoyed working amongst all men rather than all women. I enjoyed the job more so because I got involved in the Company Theatrical group putting on annual pantomimes and plays. Imagine me, as I never could, as the princess in Aladdin, Jack in Jack and the Beanstalk, slapping my thighs with gusto, thankfully I had spent 3 months before first night cycling like mad to try and get my fat thighs to look reasonable in tights. The cycling was done in my front room I hasten to add as it was winter. After being in the chorus and taking on choreography in Cinderella I ended up as one of the 'fat' brokers men in Puss in Boots.

Certainly felt more like me in the last one even though by now I had to wear padding. I had nightmares for weeks before the production of Aladdin as Ian at 16 and 14 year old Lisa were both on stage, and I really thought when Aladdin said "I must see this beautiful princess" the whole audience would convulse in laughter when I walked on to the stage! However, much to my surprise the video showed me as neither fat, ugly or old. So well worth a watch when I am feeling down.

I left this job when I was overlooked for promotion by a blond, blue eyed, 20 something with very little skills but a boss with a roving eye. My first experience of ageism in the workplace or could this be classed as sexual discrimination? There was no doubt I was not as 'sexy' or as young as she was.

Data Analyst/Secretary in a Public Sector office. I have no doubt there are many of you reading this who will appreciate how soul destroying it is to spend time compiling statistics only to have your boss ask you to 'massage' the figures so the region didn't look so bad and he didn't lose his job. Knowing that each Manager from the bottom up had done the same thing it is no wonder Ministers stand up in Parliament with a 'rosy' glow on how well the country is doing. He wouldn't think that if he saw the figures I produced! So with no job satisfaction I moved on again. The good thing about this job was that I accompanied one of my colleagues to assess the CV and Job Search sessions that were being run for the Government. This was the start of my interest in teaching. I think everyone should attend one of these and meet and speak to the people less fortunate than themselves. The reasons and responses to unemployment differ greatly from the different ends of the spectrum, however, one thing they all have in common is their lack of confidence in their own skills and abilities. Whether we are sacked or made redundant the same emotions are felt by everyone, albeit, in varying degrees, a feeling of worthlessness, anger, tears and in its' extreme, depression. We are our own worst enemy as it is almost impossible to bring yourself out of it. These sessions and clubs put the world into perspective and helped you to know you were not alone. Many friendships came about as like-minded individuals helped each other and quite a few set up business together.

Deciding to get away from secretarial/administration work I applied for a job as a Sales and Marketing Assistant at a 5 star hotel. A complete change for me having to dress in power suits and have lunches and dinners with clients. My people skills came in very handy and as far as sales went I found that I had a knack for this type of work. Initially the hotel was undergoing a major rebuilding and repairs programme, so taking prospective clients around the hotel meant wearing lovely suits, wellington boots and hard hats. Very swish! I eventually had to leave as I was unable to fulfil all the nightly social events due to family pressures and a new girl was brought in who was single and free. I became the 'lacky' answering the phones and sending out marketing letters, not what I wanted to do at all so a few months later I moved on.

I would also like to mention I was already becoming frustrated before the events with the new girl transpired. I had sold a weekend of venue, bedrooms, special dinners and nights in the nightclub, to a well-known European Media company who usually placed their conferences in London. If this one worked he would place all his business with our hotel as we had access to a harbour, marina, airport and a direct train from London. I made sure all the relevant departments were briefed and emphasised with the heads of each department how important this business could be to the hotel. Much to my disgust, and the company of course, the rooms were not ready, builders were banging all day disrupting their meetings, special wine ordered was not available on the first night. The different department heads were called to account as of course the company informed them they would never place any future business with the Hotel. Guess what? The housekeeping staff were blamed for the rooms not being ready, the builders couldn't care less, and ultimately the wine waiter was blamed for the non-purchase of the special wine. It was then that I realised that no-one takes responsibility for errors, especially if they are jumped up waiters in livery who have managed to progress to management of their respective departments. How a business can run like that was a major shock to me, but as the time went on, this incident was just the first of many!

I persuaded a major car leasing company from London to hold their annual sales conference at the Hotel. The main selling point was the ability to drive the cars into the large conference room. The organiser was over the moon as this would work as an incentive to his sales force. Unfortunately 1 week before the conference the Hotel Manager decided to give away the room and moved them to another one, where they were unable to bring in their cars. Fighting my corner was a complete waste of time and needless to say the Leasing company were less than impressed with either the hotel, staff or management.

During this period my boss and I were targeted to get £10 million of business for the coming year to which I contributed at least 25% of that. But what is the point when these ended up all one offs with no repeat business.

While the hotel was being rebuilt around us there was minimum staffing levels, so I was asked to support HR and the interviews, which I was happy to do. Firstly the HR Manager hired an assistant, very pretty, lots of make up, but a girl who found it extremely difficult to understand confidentiality in her role. We hired some 200 staff in the next couple of months, all with 5 star credentials. The Management managed to lose the majority of these staff within a couple of months, having to recruit those less qualified. This came about because the staff were fed cold sandwiches, morning, noon and night, as the kitchens had not been completed. When you have staff running up and down the back stairs of a 6 storey hotel, taking crockery up to the 6th floor and then back down again when the kitchens were ready, how can you expect to keep them when they are treated so appallingly.

I lost my dedicated parking space, free lunch in the hotel next door, and of course my credibility with the customers I had dealt with.

During the re-opening of the hotel we were expecting a visit from a dignitary for the official ceremony and security was supposedly beefed up. Amazingly D'Artagnan, calling to see me in his work clothes, was not stopped once, but I was stopped every time I moved around the hotel.

Not sure which direction to go next I agreed to help D'Artagnan promote and grow his business. Flushed with my sales success at the hotel I went in with both feet. Designing marketing material and finding ways to reach my market was inspiring and challenging. Of all my family I was the least creative so the fact that my leaflets worked was a real boost to my self-esteem. Sales flooded in and D'Artagnan set about expanding the workforce, vans and equipment.

New things I did learn when setting up your own business, watch out you don't get caught in the VAT trap, the absolute bane of my life filling out VAT forms. Don't on any account rely on your Accountant to get it right as his £200 mistake led to an unwelcome investigation from the tax man. Months of meetings where I sat piggy in the middle giving answers to either my husband or the accountant as the tax man would not acknowledge me at all. Not sure what that was about, but what a farce to end up paying the tax man £50 and an additional £750 accountant's bill on top of the bill already paid for the accounts, which he got wrong! A lesson learned never to sign off your accounts without understanding them! I wonder to this day why we are forced to use accountants that will not take any responsibility for their own mistakes.

One accountant, which I changed quickly, spent 1 hour looking for a 2p error in my accounts, while I sat there, repeatedly telling him I would give him the 2p, but oh no, as the accountant mentality took over, he kept going until he found it! He even managed to raise a little 'whoop' which I found extremely irritating as it had cost me an hour of his time!

I eventually returned to paid employment after 5 years as I realised that we were working 24/7 and having to deal with irate customers complaining about our young apprentices playing cowboys in the wood, swimming in the pool, or playing chase on the rooftops. Add to that the amount of repairs on the vans we had to undertake. Taking on apprentices was a good idea in D'Artagnan's line of work as he needed to train them to do the job properly. After a year the best of the lads got a van, all the equipment to do the job, and a decent salary. I think by then D'Artagnan was relieved to take charge of his own company again and not have to listen to my constant 'nagging'.

It is interesting to note that at some stage during my marriage D'Artagnan asked me to stop nagging, I fought my corner saying that I felt it was reminding and not nagging, however, I stopped. After a couple of months of missing appointments, turning up late, or not remembering to do things, he asked me to start again! Worth a try if you have the same problem.

The overriding reason was really because we both found that although we had more money, we had less time for our personal relationship and we did little else except talk business, row about the kids, even to the extent that it was affecting our friendship and sex life and that was a definite no no if we were to stand any chance of our relationship lasting.

Administrator at a large car company - After several fruitless interviews I managed to get a job in the IT department and it was this job that was to shape the rest of my career until retirement.

I learnt to use and build computers and found that the job utilised many of the previous skills I had developed. It was here that I met a lovely lady who was the senior IT Trainer for the company and we became friends. When she was promoted to Manager of the department she encouraged me to take on the role of IT trainer and taught me so many of the skills to become a confident and successful trainer. I suppose the most interesting part of the job was when I was asked to put together and deliver a team building course for the department. The department included software analysts, developers, technicians and a company help desk all of them unaware of the responsibilities of each other with the consequence that the staff worked in isolation affecting the productivity and efficiency of support to the company.

This was my first opportunity to prove my worth and was a challenge to beat all others as I was presented with a hostile class and a belligerent Senior IT trainer who felt aggrieved that he had not been asked to run the course. No-one except my boss, and of course me, could see the value of what we were going to try and achieve. My boss decided to release the staff for one afternoon a week for as long as the course lasted.

I started by telling them all that this course would last as long as the 'group' wanted it to, or for the course length of 8 weeks, but that it had to be a unanimous decision. Each week I would get the group together giving them the basic skills and setting them individual and group tasks necessary to get them thinking as a team. Each week I asked them if they wished to continue and their enthusiasm and keenness to continue took both me and my boss by surprise. After 6 weeks the Company decided the course could no longer continue, at which time they all fought against that decision and wanted to complete the course, even my most belligerent attendee!

I can honestly say that the atmosphere and working practices improved within the department.

I tried to bring the same idea to my last Trainer job without success. Some bosses are just unable to see the wood for the trees and there is little you can do about that other than put up with it or leave.

IT Trainer for local Further Education college and Prison. Having been made redundant from the Car company and going through all the usual emotions that come with being thrown out on your ear, I managed to get a job carrying out software training for all age groups with all levels of experience, from basic computing to City and Guilds for the local Further Education College.

I absolutely loved this job as I was asked to set up a satellite IT training centre. What joy, using all those skills I had learnt from all my previous jobs, setting up a business from scratch, marketing, logistics, planning, admin, dealing with people and of course the training itself. I did give up teaching in the prison after a year as I felt more like a gaoler than a teacher and was never sure whether the inmates were there to learn or just look at my legs. Nice for my confidence though that even over the age of 40 there were still some who wanted to look, albeit they were a captive audience and didn't get a lot of choice!

The best thing I did working for Further Education was to study for my PGCE teaching qualification which took 2 years and gave me the opportunity to put the things I learned immediately into practice.

Eventually work dried up as funding stopped and the centre was closed. I did go into mainstream college but found the new requirements on course content just too restrictive and time consuming.

Undertaking teacher jobs in other colleges also came to an abrupt end due to funding, for which I was grateful. I found myself trying to teach computing to ethnic students who had no command of English. Luckily a couple of the women did the translating, very difficult if they were both off at the same time. It was certainly a challenge, although in the end it was my decision to leave. I was asked to change all my exercises and methods of teaching to include basic English grammar and Mathematics. Even this would have been difficult with a class of English people, but almost impossible with non-English speakers. I decided I was neither an English or Maths teacher!

Looking for work I got a position as a 'supply' IT Trainer at a secondary school and failed miserably! I had gone in with such high hopes, attending 2 weeks of unpaid time to learn the school systems and attend a few of those 'incept' days. I prepared the lesson plans, worked out how I was going to deliver effective training to the different age groups, and went in on my first morning, not exactly confident, but at least not quivering with fear!

The most disconcerting thing I found was the school Incept Day. I attended a session held for all teachers which seemed to be covering new methods of teaching different subjects. All covered in my PGCE some years ago as the basic. No wonder our schools are failing!

Unfortunately for me, and I am not making up excuses to cover for my failure, it went downhill from the moment I stepped into the staff room where I was given advice on how to manage a class of 28. I just wish I hadn't listened and had started as I wanted as the advice which I followed just managed to get me off on the wrong foot with the class. Promised teaching resources were not available or not working and added to this was a last minute change to the subject I was to deliver to all the classes. So with no resources and little confidence in what I was doing meant 12 weeks later I was still spending 30 minutes of every class on behaviour management and gave it up as a lost cause.

When I say behaviour management, imagine this – you have a class of 28, half want to listen and learn and the other half want to chat, play on their mobiles and send emails! When I told one lad to stop doing his emails and get on with the work he should be doing, he said I had no right to stop him. I warned him 3 times and then turned his computer off. His response was how was he going to learn now, so I told him from next week he could start learning as long as he came into class with a better attitude.

The worst thing about this school was that every morning I was handed a sheet about the students and things I should be aware of. A sample of these were: Be kind to Jimmy as he has just broken up with his long time girlfriend (he was 11 years old)! Do not sit student A next to student B because they don't like each other. Jenny and Jane have had a fall out in the playground, so keep them apart. To be honest by the end of the first week I still didn't know who was who, so avoiding the issues was a minefield.

I tried name tags but that didn't work with one class as they gleefully swapped badges when I wasn't looking. One of the remedial classes, a girl threw her name badge on the floor saying she would not wear it. OK, so for the next hour I called everyone by their name and chatted with them, and every time I came to her I apologised for not knowing who she was and didn't bother with the chat. Believe it or not at the end of the class she stayed behind and apologised. Mind you the amount of pornography these 11 year olds were passing around the network and printing out in beautiful colour made me just shudder.

There was some good things, especially the 6 formers, who had 2 lessons with me, one during school hours and one after. My mentor had told me not to expect them after school and much to her amazement they all turned up ready to work every week.

I came out of there with my confidence well and truly battered. I now have great respect for anyone who takes up a teaching profession with children and sticks with it.

I attended loads of interviews with Recruitment Agencies (waste of space and time), and jobs that I turned down for one reason or another. In fact one interview I attended, the gentleman, and I use this term loosely, proceeded to ask me questions about who wore the trousers in my family and did my husband not feel intimidated by my skills and confidence. I told him to stick the job and walked out mid interview. It is a real shame that Managers are not trained with interview skills! I even offered him a training course to which he, shocked and affronted that he should even consider it, willingly showed me the door.

At least after all my years experiencing different interview techniques, good and bad, I didn't let it knock me down at all!

One job I went for was looking for an administrator in the IT department only to find when I got there that I would be expected to run the department in the absence of my boss who spent about 6 months of the year overseas. Overtime (no extra pay) was expected so I was pleased when I got a letter saying thanks but no thanks and I didn't have to make the choice. I watched this job being advertised continually over the next 2 years and believe it or not they eventually phoned me and asked if I was still looking for a job as they would be interested in hiring me! Of course by then I had got another job, but then what did they expect, that I was sitting around for 2 years just waiting for them to decide I was the right person for the job!

IT Trainer for a small software development company. I got this job as they were looking for a professional trainer to take on the training that had been undertaken in the past by unqualified staff. They had identified that this was a major failing for the business. For the first 6 years I revelled in being able to use all my past skills in one job with the backing of the Director who let me get on with setting up the training and resources. To this day I have only received a half dozen bad feedback reports, mainly caused by the software, bad networks or bad training venues - all of which were out of my control.

However, I have never worked in such a disorganised and 'busy', (self inflicted), company before and find it frustrating that simple ideas brought to the table, when asked for, are dismissed out of hand. Funnily enough some of these were implemented but it seems only when one of the male employees thought it was a good idea?

All in all, I loved the training and that part of my job has been so fulfilling. As I was the only trainer for this company my job was to travel around the UK delivering user, management and technical training to the staff of Public Services and Charities who had bought our software. Planning and preparation were an essential part of my role, organising the right type of venues, equipment and levels of competency. All of which contribute to successful training and learning.

What actually happened on numerous occasions was that I would turn up to find the venue less than adequate. Once I ended up on a landing with a two seater settee, one small table under a window with no blinds and a side wall to project the screen from my laptop. On seeing this I advised that this was not conducive to training, but they insisted. So you can imagine, no place for me to sit, 6 members of staff sitting on the sofa, 3 on the seat and 3 on the back. The sun shining onto the wall screen, and my laptop screen being almost too small to see from my standpoint. Then there was the time I turned up in Wales, imagine the travel time, to find a room with no network, no PCs or laptops, and evidently no-one taking responsibility. By that time I said my piece on my expectations and went out to the garden to have a coffee and wait. This meant that starting nearly 2 hours later than anticipated they complained that there had not been enough time and the training was rushed!

Then there were the venues that were just a real pleasure. I spent a week in Cardiff, Wales at a super IT training venue, where everything was set up and ready, including coffee. I had 4 groups over the week and by the end the venue organisers stopped me just as I was leaving on the Friday evening to go home. She said to me "Was that IT training you were doing this week"? I confirmed and she followed up with "I have never in all my years seen a bunch of students coming out of IT training absolutely buzzing with what a great week it had been"! It's those types of comments that made the rest of my job with the company worthwhile.

Then there are the times when you turn up for training to find a mixed ability class, by that I mean, some could use a computer and others didn't know the basics of how a mouse worked! This of course adds to the complexity of training, trying to cover the course content in the time given and still manage to teach the non PC literate ones a crash course in using a computer. It didn't seem to matter how often I emphasised the need for similar IT skill levels they still insisted on just squeezing in one or 2 that needed extra help! In turn that would mean my feedback forms almost always included one or two comments of "the training was too fast". Sometimes you just can't win!

I have many happy memories and good and bad experiences over the years, including those I came across as a lone woman in a hotel. Over the years I have been asked to visit a policeman's room, been joined at every meal by a philanderer intent on getting me into his bed, and a hotel manager who upgraded my room and then thought that gave him the right to bang on my door at 11pm at night just to make sure I was OK. Once in my door it took me a while to get him to leave, until eventually I told him to back off or I would get him arrested for harassment.

Staying in different hotels and B&Bs gave me an insight into the good and bad and what the blurb on their web site actually means. One lovely hotel had peacocks wandering around the grounds. Lovely you think until you find 2 standing outside your bedroom door and just won't let you out! The best ones are the large anonymous ones with a spa and a decent menu. Those didn't always come together, but after a day's fractious training, a swim and a sauna are a boon.

Once I stayed in a small B&B (booked by the company I was training) only to find no lock on my door and I was expected to join the family for meals. An extremely large married couple and Father who managed to dish up the most enormous meals, not on the table to help yourself, but on a very large plate. They were most disappointed that I couldn't manage to eat more than a quarter, while they tucked into and cleared their plates.

Teaching software is not always as easy as it sounds, especially when the software invariably didn't work to specification and had error messages by the dozen. The first error message, sometimes while just trying to log in was a good teaching technique, showing the students how the errors were dealt with and methods for getting round them. However, after 12 in succession at one venue, the Manager who had been reluctant to have the software in the first place, complained vociferously throughout the 2 days training. Even though I had offered to postpone the training and return at a future date. It was this one that led to my final redundancy from this company.

After going through 5 redundancy rounds in the 9 years I was employed with the company and managing to hold on to my job, the last but one redundancy saw me restricted to a 3 day week, which at the time suited me fine. Unfortunately during those 3 years the Company went through 2 more redundancy rounds and although saved the first time I decided by the second, enough was enough. Please do read about my experiences with this company in my Workplace Bullying chapter.

It just amazes me that anyone can run a company based on fear and intimidation, using regular redundancies to get rid of staff that just didn't fit in with his ideas, and ultimately save him the bother of verbal warnings, written warnings and all the paraphernalia needed to sack someone! Always it was someone who stood up to him that faced the chop!

Full-time Carer - Redundancy from my previous job meant a re-think for both me and D'Artagnan. Mother-in-Law's (Jemima) health had deteriorated and it was evident that she needed full time care now. So it did seem logical that my new job should be that of full-time carer and

D'Artagnan would continue to work. I was now eligible for my pension and between us we could just about manage.

I had been looking after Jemima since she came to live with us and as time progressed we brought in part-time carers while I was at work for 3 days as her needs grew and her abilities diminished.

The first thing to do was to sort out the finances, cut down on expenses and adjust to the new life which was going to affect us all. Adding stair and bath lifts, baby monitor and wheelchair as the need arose.

It has certainly been challenging and although easy at the beginning has now become a lot more difficult as her dementia progresses. I now work harder than ever before, every day is a challenge.

Duties are as diverse as you can imagine. Initially it was just making sure that Jemima had the help she needed with dressing, washing, health and taking her to a weekly dementia group. I also had to take her with me wherever I went as she could not be left at home on her own. Now there is so much more as her dementia takes it's emotional toll on us all.

I am of course not dealing with this alone as D'Artagnan takes his turn to look after her and give me time off. This is usually an hour or two some days when she has returned to bed and I go up the park walking, running and exercising, acknowledging the fact that at 64 years old unless I keep fit, the general moving of Jemima around the house will be impossible.

As dementia is such a big subject I have written a chapter on Alzheimers/ Dementia where you can follow Jemima's and our trials and tribulations whilst dealing with this debilitating disease. I have also added a chapter on my duties as a Carer.

Writing (I hesitate to call myself an author)

This has been my project since before retiring. I spent almost a year with the idea and then on the concept of how I could present my story before even starting to write. Starting at the beginning I wrote an outline for each of the proposed chapters and then asked Caroline to read it to see whether it was worth my while progressing with it. I have never been creative so her input was important. Her encouragement has been invaluable, as have the input from a couple of friends and associates. Everyone told me they couldn't stop reading it but felt that they wanted more detail, so the last 2 years have been spent digging around in my memory to include this without losing the way I wanted to express myself.

I hope I have managed to achieve this and that I will manage to reach the end of the book and get it published and appreciated while still alive rather than posthumously! Time will tell!

I love writing and hope that this will be my last job of work as I love retirement and dread ever having to go back into the rat race of structured employment.

You never know, maybe I have more than one book in me!

WORKPLACE HARASSMENT AND BULLYING

It seems an ideal place to follow on with this chapter as I have over my working life encountered so many different types of harassment or bullying and the workplace is very different from the childish bullying I encountered in my early years as so much more has to be considered when trying to deal with it.

I was very lucky with my jobs until I was in my 30s when I realised that harassment/bullying comes in so many different forms and levels.

The odious boss I had at the Pharmaceutical company was one in a million, at least I hope he was! Not only the constant swearing and undermining I had to contend with on a daily basis, I also had the added problem of trying to leave. I had watched him reduce a young girl to tears on a daily basis, who was determined to stick it out for a year as this was her first job. I kept telling her work should not be like this, but she held out and eventually joined me at the large corporate company. Getting back to me leaving, I arranged a meeting to discuss this with him and the minute I said I wanted to leave he walked out of the office telling me not to be so 'f.....g stupid'. I put my resignation letter on his desk and he promptly threw it in the bin, so the next morning I put the letter in his filing cabinet, which unfortunately he found and again threw away. Every morning I put a copy in the file and one on his desk until the day I left when he wouldn't even speak to me. Leaving was the only way to deal with this man and I only wish I had done it sooner.

At the large corporate car company I was continually undermined by one of my colleagues who resented me taking the job and even more so for being so successful at it. To the extent that most of the individuals seeking training would opt for me first. It took me quite a while to work out that he was sabotaging me by changing settings and passwords on the computers so I would look silly or have to seek his help. Nothing that I could prove of course and his behaviour continued with all his dealings with me, being unhelpful and some instances just downright rude.

My answer to this was to tell my boss, who understood, but agreed that we needed to have a strategy in place to deal with it. This started with checking everything before starting training to ensure it was all set and working correctly and to get someone else to help me rectify anything I couldn't personally deal with. To put all requests in writing in order to prompt a written answer (which meant the rudeness was gone) and generally just not to take it personally. With the backing of my boss and her appreciation of the good job I was doing was enough to make my life and job bearable. To this day I still think this man had problems with women in the workplace and no doubt he still does! Having an understanding boss willing to stand by you goes a long way and definitely kept me in this job longer than I would have done without her support. We are still in touch and I continue to thank her for the support and training she gave me that I believe has made me the excellent trainer I am today. My feedback forms attest to this so not just my word on it!

My last job at the software development company - I had been with the company some 9 years and for the last 3 years my job had been a nightmare and the cause of me having to resort to taking 'happy pills' just so I don't throw myself in front of a train, punch my Director or walk out of the job. So close to retirement I decided to just hang on and for the first time in my life, work for the money!

What happened to change my job was a general redundancy that the Company decided was necessary during the economic crisis in 2012. We were all asked to either request early redundancy or come up with some ideas to minimise costs. Being a small close knit workforce and all loyal to the Company we all came up with suggestions that were never discussed again or even taken up. I was asked if I would consider a 3 day week or a change in my job. I didn't want to change from being a Trainer but offered suggestions for 3 days training and 2 days support. When it came to the final meeting I was offered the 3 day week or leave!

I couldn't fit all my work in a 5 day week let alone a 3 day one, but his answer was to take away elements of my job and give these to other colleagues in the office, and this in turn made my job even harder. They were themselves already overworked and this led to resentment towards me by my colleagues. I found this especially difficult as he did not tell me he had given a part of my job to a colleague and it was some weeks before I realised, mainly from the way my colleagues treated me. He had also convinced them that I would be difficult if they told me themselves, so they all felt they were walking on egg shells whenever I was in the office. When I did find out I hastily apologised to my colleagues for inadvertently, in some cases, stepping on their toes! My boss deliberately excluded me from all customer meetings, talking to customers about support, and consequently I was unable to drum up business for a training room that he had set up at our offices. I asked for a marketing budget, but he said no, he would deal with that and didn't. Then I was blamed that the venture had not been a success.

I managed to get him to agree to lieu time as my job took me all round the country and that meant unsociable and long hours. He wouldn't ever pay me for the lieu time and was resentful when I took it. One day he took me out of the office for a coffee and told me he could not support my lieu hours anymore as he was finding it extremely difficult to justify my absences from the office to the rest of the staff. I fought my corner and told him if he stopped my lieu hours then I would only work the hours he paid me for, 9 to 5. This would mean no more travelling at 6 o'clock in the morning to get to run a training course from 9 til 5 and then travel back, arriving home at sometimes 10 or 11 at night. This would affect the amount of training I could undertake in my 3 days to one a week rather than the 3 I was currently fitting in. I was taking my lieu and holiday time to fit in with the customer needs, so he needed to be more flexible with my times. Eventually he agreed with me to continue the lieu hours, but this was just to be another nail in my coffin and would be used against me at a future date. I was determined to hang on or hope he offered me redundancy at which point I would jump at the chance.

From that day on my boss no longer spoke to me or answered my emails and the agreed 6 monthly review just did not happen over the next 2 years. My first review was spent on the stairs for 3 minutes when I asked what his plans were and was told I was to continue on the 3 day week. During this time he had agreed to set up a static training room in our offices and had given the task to the administrator. So the room was set up with no consultation with me until I complained about the chairs she had ordered. An IT room with chairs and no wheels or height adjustment? I had to fight my corner with Health and Safety regulations before I got my way. Other than that, any other suggestions I offered were ignored and I was told that was the way it was going to be as they had already made the decisions.

I loved delivering the training but hated every minute spent in the office. No longer did I try to have meetings with him, or complain about my lot, and just spent time saying OK to whatever he came up with. I have learnt that there is no point in having an opinion or complaining as nothing is ever listened to or dealt with. I think there was an element of sexual discrimination going on as the women in the company seemed to be having similar problems with their male counterparts, however, I didn't have any proof other than the fact that all the women complained of being ignored or side-lined in favour of a male associate.

Although I still don't know for sure what changed his opinion of me or why our close working relationship died it was evident from my last redundancy meeting with him that he had his reasons. These appeared in essence to be complaints he had received from customers in the past. When I asked him why he had not taken me to task on these complaints and given me a chance to rectify or improve whatever it was, he told me he had dealt with them when they arose. Why had he set me up to fail by not telling me about this I can only assume that he was looking for an excuse to get rid of me and he was just biding his time. My immediate thought was to take him to court for sexual discrimination and Unfair Dismissal but ultimately this was not a route I decided to take.

On speaking to ACAS, which is the supposedly independent employer/employee mediator, who advised that as far as they were concerned there was no proof and he could not be penalised for being a bad boss! He had followed the correct/legal process for redundancy. I then went to the Citizen Advice Bureau and spoke to one of their solicitors who put it quite succinctly and made my decision for me.

Do you want to fight through the courts for the next 7-10 years?

Do you want to remain in contact with your Boss for the next 7-10 years?

Do you want your job back?

Are you seeking compensation?

The answer to all 4 of these questions was NO, NO, NO, NO! So like a lot of employees I walked away.

The most amazing discrimination I have met in almost all of my jobs has been as a result of my efficiency. I have always tried to do any job I undertake to the best of my ability and apparently this 'frightens' my bosses and causes resentment with my colleagues. Why, I don't know, as I would have thought any boss that takes you on to do a job would be over the moon that you were good at it! Eventually I consciously changed the way I dealt with my colleagues and work. No longer did I come up with answers to questions asked or contribute to company discussions or meetings unless specifically asked. I suppose what I was doing now was 'hiding my light under a bushel' as the saying goes.

Unfortunately this did have an adverse effect on my natural instincts and I had to change who I am and this leads to resentment, stress and a lack of interest in the job. If I hadn't been so close to retirement and fearful of ever getting another job I am sure I would have been out of the door!

Dealing with any type of discrimination in the workplace is fraught with dangers not only to your career but your home life too. No-one should have to put up with it and I know that laws are in place now to help you deal with it, but ultimately if you bring it out into the open your life at work can be hell and if you don't bring it out into the open both you and your home life suffer.

So if you are not as old as I am you should not put up with it and if you don't feel strong enough to deal with it and try and keep your job, then get another one and leave as soon as possible. From my experience these people don't change and are rarely to blame. They are the ones that get the salary increases and keep their jobs! Get out as soon as you can!

I made a big mistake in my choice to stay on with this company when I was forced into the 3 day week. In retrospect I should have left then and would have avoided 3 years of a boss treating me badly with all the consequent stress, anxiety, lack of confidence and general unhappiness in my job.

Your own personal circumstances of course have a direct influence on how you can deal with a problem in the workplace. For me, my age was a contributing factor, and I did not want to end up taking any job just for the sake of it, when for me, training was my joy! In the end I had the most miserable 3 years of my life and now realise that anything would have been better than putting up with the treatment I received from my boss and some of my colleagues. This led to me doubting my own abilities and character. He managed to convince me that I was not a nice person, my colleagues hated me, and ultimately the training I delivered, (which he had never complained about in a total of 9 years), suddenly was not up to standard!

It took me nearly 2 years to deal with this mentally and to become the confident person I believed myself to be before that dreaded last redundancy. I now realise that I was not at fault, I did do my job well, and the problem was his not mine! My expectations of customer satisfaction with his products was far higher than his, which led to more confrontations than he could deal with. Well that is what I tell myself every day!

LIVING WITH
ALZHEIMER'S / DEMENTIA

Since becoming a full-time carer for my Mother-in-Law, Jemima, I have seen firsthand just how dreadful this disease can be not only for the sufferer but also for family members. Watching it progress from the early stages over a period of 12+ years and in particular watching how she has coped with it has been a real eye-opener. Reading up on the subject shows that the effect and progression is very different for everyone so whatever you read can only be a guideline. However it does give you a good insight on what is likely to happen and the many ways there are of dealing with the different stages.

In Jemima's case it started in her mid 80's and developed very slowly with short term memory loss in the initial stages followed by a general confusion with understanding what was being said to her and her own ability to communicate with others. These early stages led to us seek help through the GP to have an assessment carried out by the local dementia clinic. At that time she was diagnosed with on-set age related dementia.

The assessment itself was a real hoot, if I can dare to say that, as Jemima's spirit has always been there right from the start and is still very much in evidence. When asked to remember an address her response was "Why would I want to do that". It seemed strange to her to be asked to remember a fictitious address to which she would have no use. When asked to remember a fruit and he would ask her in 5 minutes what that fruit was her response was "What fruit? What are you talking about"!

To deal with this memory and communication problem as it progressed she would automatically turn to me for the answers rather than have the stress of trying to remember or deal with a question. At the beginning I found myself taking on that role, which is so very easy to do. However, I realised that as long as I was answering for her then her mind would deteriorate quicker. So early on I would use prompts to help her remember and used keywords to help her communicate. I insisted that the GP or any other people addressed themselves to her and not automatically to me, again prompting her to give her own answers whatever they may be. Going to see her GP can be difficult as her instant response when asked how she is, she will say she is fine. "No I don't have a pain there", when you are there to get them to sort out a pain in her stomach. Of course in the later stages we have had some interesting and amusing responses and incidents that somehow show us that she is still there in spirit. She has always had a quirky sense of humour and although this isn't as often now it is always a pleasure for us when it shines through.

With the general health problems that are associated with age, Jemima had fallen over in the bathroom and managed to split her head open. The ambulance men arrived and immediately she was flirting outrageously with them. Once in the hospital she loudly questioned the A&E doctor's qualifications to deal with the cut on her head. Had he been trained in the army or not! The young nurses and doctors were overwhelmed by how stoic she was while they prodded, poked and sewed up her cut. As she told them, "When you've been in a war this is nothing to cry about"!

The real frustration for Jemima over the years has been her ability to know that something is not right. Early on knowing that the words she uses are not the right ones. She would search her mind looking for those elusive words and often her sentences would be difficult to understand. However hard she tries the words just will not come and even when prompted with the right word she will not recognise it. D'Artagnan and I do have fun trying to work out what it is exactly that she is asking for. Over time it does become easier especially if you keep to a routine as much as possible and knowing Jemima so well has helped considerably.

Her short term memory loss at the beginning was easy to deal with and her acceptance of this was not so traumatic as it was to become later on. We would talk extensively with her on the areas of her life that she did remember, answering only the questions she would ask on the things that had happened during her 'missing' years. However, being aware of these blanks in her memory, Jemima began to fight against the answers, often refusing point blank that she had ever been married. My own thoughts are that these memories were not good ones for Jemima, so her mind naturally blocked these out, as she didn't want to remember them.

Jemima loves singing and I have made it part of our life whether at home, in the car or just walking around the supermarket. Her mind, I am sure has been better for it as whatever her vocabulary is like she always remembers the words to the songs we sing. We have a lot of 'la la la' songs. These are the ones where neither of us can remember a line, and this she finds amusing and refers to as our la la songs.

The hardest thing for the family is the knowledge that one day she will not recognise us at all. I am sure you can all imagine how hurtful this can be, but it is Jemima who suffers the most. She hates not knowing where she is and who the people are around her. She is often anxious and frightened and this only gets worse for her as the disease progresses.

D'Artagnan is her one constant once she accepts that he exists, although at times we have to laugh, especially when she walks up to him in the kitchen, taps him on the shoulder, and says "Do you know where my son is"?. Once when he said that he was her son, she responded with "No you're not, you're an old man"! Understandable when her memory of him is when he was a child. Still she does remember to check with him before going out that he has a vest and hat on and that he is to take care. Hard for him to get used to being treated like an 11 year old all over again.

Dealing with all the changes is difficult and often frustrating especially now that I spend every day repeating the same information to her as to where she is, who I am, where her family is, and how she came to be where she is today. The hardest thing to do is fighting the urge to say "I told you before" or "We talked about this yesterday, don't you remember". I fill in the blanks as often as she needs them filled. We laugh together every time she asks who I am and I respond with" That's me". I used to say "I'm Robyn", but unfortunately she took that phrase as my name and there were now two Robyns.

More upsetting for me over the past couple of years has been this confusion over the two me's. One she tells me is bossy, thinks she owns and knows everything, and she doesn't like her at all. Whenever we go anywhere or do anything she asks me to ensure that I have cleared it with 'I'm Robyn', just in case we get into trouble. I worked out that the 'I'm Robyn' is the one that is downstairs and does all the rushing about, cooking, cleaning etc and the 'Robyn' is the one that is upstairs caring for her needs and giving her undivided attention. Her moods are often dictated by which Robyn she thinks she is with and her jealousy when I am busy or talking with other people are very marked by the sarcasm and short answers I get from her.

Of course at the age she is now there is so much more to consider other than the dementia. She has arthritis in both knees and suffers dreadfully with the pain. D'Artagnan and I have spent the last five years trying to find a combination of pain relief medication that works for her.

One thing is evident, the skin irritation that she constantly suffered with was caused by several of the available pills the Doctor tried with her. Driving not only her mad but our attempts to offset the irritation was time consuming and overwhelming both day and night.

Eventually we were driven to consider the stronger drugs available such as morphine, but the change in her mental capacity was frightening. Almost overnight she became almost catatonic, couldn't speak, couldn't carry out the easiest of functions that she could normally do, such as bathing, holding a spoon or in fact knowing what the spoon was for. She lost a tremendous amount of weight and it was difficult in the end to see where the dementia started and the side effects of morphine took over.

Taking the bull by the horns I took her off all her medication, with the agreement of her doctor, and the fact that Jemima had refused to take all medication at that time, I gave only paracetamol for her knees for the next 4 weeks. Within days Jemima was back to her 'normal' self but suffering more with the arthritis in her knees. After a discussion with my sister, who has arthritis, and the drug she has prescribed, we researched other available arthritic drugs on the Internet and found that the specific drug she had told us about showed good results. Speaking to the doctor we were told that this was not prescribed for over 65's due to the added risk of heart attack or stroke. Both D'Artagnan and I felt that at her age whatever she did gave her those risks, yet still they would not prescribe it for her.

Caroline was coming over at Christmas and after speaking to her doctor brought over a week's supply, which we tried. The pain although not completely gone was a lot more manageable and instead of taking pills 4 times a day, this was one liquid dose in 24 hours and NO side effects!

After further discussions with her doctor and showing him the results of our trial he agreed to prescribe this drug for her. As with all drugs over the months we have increased the dosage, but again with no side effects.

At 96 she is still walking albeit with a walking frame, walking stick or my arm. She still helps with the drying up after dinner, washes and feeds herself. It has been an uphill struggle for us all but I do recommend researching and fighting for what you believe is right for your relative. You know them far better than any hospital, community nurse or doctor. Although the current drugs are working for Jemima, the stories I see and hear from other carers is that what works for one dementia patient does not necessarily work for another. Much depends on the other medical conditions your relative might be suffering with and these medications may well conflict. So I don't advocate that you should follow my example but wanted only to share our experiences that might just give your family added hope that sometimes changing the medication might just improve the quality of life for your relative and ultimately the whole family.

The one thing I do try to do is to take Jemima out of the house to do things she likes doing. At the start of her rapid decline I took her to a Tea Dance. She has always loved to dance and although I do this at home with her it is never satisfying, especially as I can't even waltz. Anyway, after a fractious morning of trying to get her dressed, off we went, and her face was a picture when I took her in to the hall. The lights were pretty, the organ playing was just at the right volume and the dancers on the floor took her back to her teen years. We jived, we waltzed and had tea and cake. By the end of the afternoon even I could waltz after a fashion. The fact that Jemima forgot the event almost within hours wasn't important, it was still definitely worth the effort. Her smile is worth a thousand hard days.

I also took her to a coffee lounge on the seafront and amazingly she thought she was back at her childhood home in the North of England. We had a lovely couple of hours while she pointed out landmarks and talked about her days on the beach and where she lived. As the weather improves I hope that I can get her dressed and take her back there. If only I had known that there was no need to stress myself about my inability to take her back to her childhood town, it was just down the road!

Aggression is one of the later expected symptoms of dementia and we have seen this in Jemima. The very upsetting screaming and shouting in the middle of the night and the resultant physical aggression is very frightening. This is a very distressing, tiring, embarrassing and difficult symptom of the disease to deal with.

The aggression increased relatively quickly and was almost constant, both verbally and physically. Last night she wrecked her bedroom and both D'Artagnan and I spent a couple of hours trying to get her washed and dressed. The incontinence can be dealt with easily when the person is willing, but when they are not it can deteriorate rapidly into a war of wills. From the recent binging on anything and everything 24 hours a day, she now refuses to eat or drink. Even the taking of her medication has become difficult, so her knees suffer more than ever. I am amazed that Jemima manages to hide her pills in her mouth, secreting them in her hankie or spitting them onto the floor. We have come to the conclusion that our attempts to crush her pills and put them in her meals is the reason she had stopped eating. She was convinced that we were poisoning her and questions regularly whether she could trust us with her food.

One day I was with Jemima and helped her out of the car to put her in the disabled trolley to go shopping in the supermarket when she suddenly started yelling at the top of her voice "Help, help" followed by a piercing scream and stiffened her legs and arms to stop me putting her in the trolley. I just thanked my lucky stars that we were in the car park and not in the middle of the supermarket.

To help Jemima with her knees we would regularly exercise to music and do exercises every morning. Unfortunately this is becoming more difficult to do with her current concentration levels, but I persevere when she lets me! Now she is walking less and resting more I worry less about this.

Initially we researched options from the Internet where we found Bio-Melatonin and have tried this with Jemima. The affect was marginal so we approached both the Alzheimer's support and the Doctor to try and get us all through this traumatic time and hopefully the new liquid sleeping medicine, Lorazepam, will do the job.

Thanks to the Memantine prescribed by the Alzheimer Clinic there has been no repetition of her aggression, not that I am convinced that this behaviour has gone forever. Although this does not work for everybody it certainly did for us. I say 'us' rather than 'her' because this behaviour is something the sufferer is not aware of, however, the carer/family are the ones who have to deal with it. It does not eradicate it completely but it was a good start.

As the latter stages are becoming more evident I thought it may be useful to diarise the events, so that we can follow the progression. I have always talked about caring being a 24/7 job, but these latter stages of

Alzheimer's are particularly draining as we both try to find solutions for dealing with these events.

Jemima's decline was very quick, starting with the aggression which could come on very quickly. Usually just as you are trying to get her washed or dressed. She would acquiesce at the start but then out of the blue she would hit out either verbally or physically or both. Trying to get a pair of knickers on her has become a challenge and whether you are trying to pull them up or pull them down to go to the toilet, she will suddenly grab hold of them and fight you all the way. Her strength is amazing, considering she is just 4ft and of slight frame. So unless we have to go out and she needs to be dressed I am convinced that leaving her in her night clothes is best, as the battle morning and evening can be exhausting. Amazingly I appear more exhausted that she does!

Our 10 day diary:

DAY 1 - we noticed a rapid deterioration that led us to consulting the doctor, Jemima had been up since 6am and we had gone down to breakfast. First the cup of tea was thrown all over me as it wasn't right. Breakfast was eaten for the first few spoonfuls and then spat out at me. She spent most of the day trying to break the door down with her walking frame so she could get out of the house, asking me for a hammer once I had removed anything from the house she could possibly use. I was just impressed that she knew the right tool for the job. When I tried to stop her she proceeded to 'chase' me round the house, holding on to my shirt, pulling, pushing and hitting me. During the day her mood changes so quickly. To distract her we would sing, dance, listen to the radio and chat. By the time she went to bed that night I was worn out!

DAY 2 - the incontinence became a problem as although I had managed to get a 'nappy pant' on her she decided to pull them down and proceed to do her business on the front room floor. So now she was covered, as were her clothes and of course my floor! Trying to reason with her unsuccessfully to go upstairs for a wash we compromised that she would allow me to wash her in the kitchen. Boosted by this I ran the sink and got her washing stuff, then tried to remove her nightie and knickers. With one arm out of her nightie she suddenly decided that this was not such a good idea, so after much cajoling it ended up with me forcibly trying to strip her. She pushed against the nightie so hard that she bruised her arm in 2 places, but off it came! Next was the decidedly nasty smelling nappy pant, this was achieved with Jemima leaning on my back as I bent down and thumping me as hard as she could. I didn't mind a bit as after all she was no longer hanging on to the nappy pant which enabled me to get it down to her ankles. Lifting her feet was another challenge, as I do try with all my dealing with Jemima not to grab her. Reasoning with her whilst under the full weight of her body didn't work, but the fact that I just lifted her up on my back and her feet left the floor, she suddenly gave in and said "Do what you like"! If only that was true. The washing was another issue, but with perseverance, patience and the bribery of a nice cup of tea, this was all achieved in an hour and 15 minutes. By then I needed a cup of coffee! The rest of the day was spent with the alternating behaviour and her walking incessantly around the downstairs with frequent visits to her bedroom to collect nonexistent personal items such as her bag, which would be hanging round her neck at the time. Unfortunately whenever I asked her why she felt the need to go upstairs she said that was none of my business!

After today I decided to keep her in her nappy and not worry, but encouraged her to use the toilet, which she did sometimes and the rest of the time I didn't try and change her. The new nappy pants are excellent as you can rip the sides to remove them!

That night we gave her the Lorazepam instead of her usual Nitrazepam. It does take time for her to settle down but after midnight we all got a good night's sleep. We took a couple of days to get convinced to use this especially after reading the reviews from other carers who have given this to their relatives.

During the evening she spent her time waking and dozing interspersed with conversations with people in her room, sometimes lucid and sometimes in her own language. Just before I went to bed I looked in on her to find her stripped naked, upside down in her bed, feet on the wall, with her nappy pants on her head and laughing.

As hallucinations are a symptom of a urine infection we called the doctor out, who decided she needed antibiotics and took a test away to send to the pathology department.

DAY 3 - I decided to give her a the dose of Lorazepam in the morning and all in all the day was definitely better. The biggest problem I did encounter was that her balance was worse and I spent most of the day following her about to keep her safe.

Her aggression is still there but is short and sharp, she asks to go to the toilet and remains reasonable most times. Interestingly she is losing her vocabulary quite quickly and often stands talking to the wall in a language quite her own. She doesn't seem to mind so much now when she can't find the right word but we try hard to understand her when we can. She has started making up songs and these can be so interesting as something she hears or something we say will prompt her to break into song!

DAY 4 - After a fractious night Jemima eventually fell asleep to the extent that I was unable to get her up to take her to her dementia club. She woke up shouting for me to get out of her room and screaming until I left. Luckily D'Artagnan was acceptable and managed to calm her down. It is at these times that it is essential to have a second person around. Last night I was giving her a wash prior to going to bed when she suddenly turned screaming and then collapsed in a comatose state. Thankfully D'Artagnan came running and between us we managed to carry her to the bedroom. All in all a reasonable day due to the Lorazepam, although still active she doesn't seem to have the strength to manage more than a short walk or two. Still prone to the tantrums, and when I took over later in the day to give D'Artagnan time to do some work she spent most of her time giggling and putting herself on the floor. I think this was to give me something to do trying to get her back up. Overall a better day for us all. Bed by 7pm and asleep from 12am through to nearly 11:30 the following morning, for all a good night's sleep!

DAY 5 - With the late start I must admit to being a bit fearful of going into her bedroom when I woke up at 8am just in case the inevitable had happened. She was sound asleep. When waking at 11:30 she moved herself to the bottom of the bed, a place where we frequently find her. Why does it take so long to come up with a simple solution, so stark in its' simplicity that you just wonder why you didn't think of it before. My eureka moment was instead of physically moving her back to the top of the bed I have now made a top to tail bed with pillows either end. She has managed to drink a little and taken a pain killer disguised in a mashed banana, and settled down again. I have left her in her bed having managed to get her on the toilet (nothing happening there) and into a pair of warm trousers and fresh nappy pant. She is now sitting in her bed talking gobbledy gook and singing her own version of songs having ordered me out of her room! The aggression is bubbling just near the surface and I have managed to get another dose of pain killer down her disguised in her apple juice which is now her favourite drink. Now I just get sticky instead of stained with tea! A definite change for the better. Jemima decided to spend the day in her bed and although she did decide a couple of times to try and climb out together with the odd spate of anger all in all she had a better day and so did I. Now we just need to see if we can get another night's sleep!

We have decided that Lorazepam at night no longer works for Jemima as she itches constantly, so we have changed her back to her Nitrazepam at night with the Lorazepam during the day and this seems to be the answer.

Her eating patterns are transient so I feed her on demand. She eats little and often, and likes to mix the tastes. I must admit to finding things that she finds difficult to spit out at me, such as bananas, chocolates, sandwiches and cakes during the day and she eats a fresh pulverised dinner of meat/fish, potatoes and vegetables at night for dinner. This I tend to feed her with so there is less chance of me wearing it!

DAY 6 – An earlier start with call outs twice during the night for a drink and the toilet. Slept until 9am and then a day in bed on Lorazepam. I hate giving this to her as she is totally unaware of anything around her and keeps going into a comatose state whenever her brain just can't cope with what is happening around her. Whether this is when I am trying to change, wash or feed her, or loud and unfamiliar noises. Managed to get some food down her but she spent most of the day spitting it out at me and enjoying every minute of it. It is so lovely to hear her laugh that I don't mind the goo! Several shirts later she was asleep by 8pm having managed to get her Nitrazepam down her.

DAY 7 – Started Jemima on her new drug Memantine prescribed by the Alzheimer doctor. She is on a low dose which will be increased weekly over the next month. I also gave her a half dose of Lorazepam in the afternoon and the combination of both seemed to work better although she did spend the day in bed she was definitely less stressed. Nitrazepam at night and although she called me out a couple of times during the night she didn't particularly want anything except a drink and reassurance.

DAY 8 – I decided to try Jemima on just her Memantine to see what the reaction was and overall both she and I had a better day. Again spent in bed but she was more awake, we sang we chatted and generally her mood was much improved. Coming to the end of her antibiotics for her urine infection may also have contributed to her overall feeling of well being. She also came downstairs a couple of times to eat which is a major step forward for her. Another good night for us all.

DAY 9 - After the previous good day we decided to stop the Lorazepam completely and she now is on the Memantine only. Today she is more alert, her vocabulary is much improved and she has found her sense of humour. We have also managed a bath and hair wash and for the first time in a couple of weeks she has asked to get dressed and come downstairs for the afternoon. I had wanted to take her to the tea dance today and she was excited at the prospect, however, by the time I had changed her she had fallen asleep and it was too late. Much as I feel the need to escape the four walls of home I realise that it may do me good to go out but it is too early for Jemima and we settle for a sit in the garden and some singing and dancing at home.

DAY 10 – We had an early start at 6am but at least the night up until then had been quiet. After a quick non-existent wee and a drink of water she went back to sleep until 9am. Lovely! Happy most of the day with her usual bouts of anxiety. I did try to get her out for a drive but at the last minute her fear took over and so we decided not to go. I hasten to add that this was after she was in her coat, shoes, hat and gloves! She loves music so we spent a half hour listening to the radio and then she dozed.

This was her first full day just on Memantine and interestingly, her tests for a urine infection came back negative, so the hallucinations were after all part of the dementia. So difficult at times to tell the difference, but you believe your doctor don't you? Not so sure we have the faith in them that we used to. They just seem to want to reduce her medication without any thought to the consequences. Still better safe than sorry, but at least now we can find out just how she is on the Memantine. We had already found out that there was no conflict with the Italian arthritis medicine and anything else she was taking. So we think we have cracked it now.

Seven days later and on the increased dosage of Memantine the days with Jemima are a delight for all of us. She still loses words and gets frustrated with herself, but she is back to the Dementia Club and enjoying it immensely. She is once again coming shopping with me and enjoying any social visits we make. Her appetite has improved and her sleeping patterns are reasonable, although we do find that between 1am and 3am most nights she is confused, sometimes hallucinating or singing in full voice. Once settled she sleeps until about 7am.

The one drawback on the Memantine that we have discovered is her anxiety levels have increased as the afternoon progresses and she needs constant reassurance. The Memantine is increased in dose each week for 4 weeks so it is just a question of wait and see.

Once again the movement of getting Jemima indoors has resulted in a comatose state and I just can't lift her, so have spoken to the Alzheimer's nurse to see if she can put me in touch with someone who can supply us with a transit chair. Keeping my fingers crossed.

These incidences lead me to the type of equipment needed to support daily living. Besides the walker and stair lift, there are a myriad of other items to think about. We have a variety of drinking cups and plastic plates and bowls. You only really think about these last items once you have had a cup of tea thrown at you, or a bowl of porridge flung across the table. Persevere with the child cups as although struggling at first Jemima quickly learned how to suck to get what she wanted. A variety of spoons were necessary when she was feeding herself, however, when it came became evident that she was struggling to hold the spoon and it was this frustration that was leading to her throwing the food around, we now feed her. All in all she is more content during meals now knowing that she is not having to worry about it. I have often thought it would be a good idea to set up a second hand shop for all this equipment that sometimes lasts weeks rather than months, especially as the prices in the disabled shops are just so extortionate. Another one of my bug bears against the Governments' so called support for the aged and disabled. Don't get me started on the so called Age related charities and holiday firms who seem to think all older people can afford to pay double for their equipment insurance, holidays, flights etc. I just can't see why they can't put a clause in the insurance policy that says if you die of a known illness or disease, then you just get a flight home in a coffin!

Jemima loved travelling and has spent most of her last 30 years flying to SA to see her son or to Inverness to stay with her Sister-in-Law for a couple of weeks respite (for us!), both of which she loved. At the age of 85 she even went to Miami in Florida to visit her relatives. However, now due to the lack of insurance cover for a 96 year old and the fact that her last visit to SA had her held at the airport as a drug runner, her travelling days are over. I must explain that Jemima is not a drug runner but was carrying 3 months' prescription drugs in her hand luggage, together with a note from her doctor and a prescription. Evidently the SA police can't tell the difference between heroin and prescription drugs. Anyway after 4 hours in the departure lounge, not knowing what was going on, she now fears flying, thanks very much! Add to that the doctor in SA decided she had heart problems, (high blood pressure), and started her off on 10 years of taking Lisinopril, which funnily enough the doctors now decide she doesn't need to take?

Just a note about removing certain drugs, be aware that some medicines need to be weaned off, reducing the dosage over a number of weeks. For Jemima this was not necessary as she had already been some 3-4 weeks without taking medication during her aggressive period. So the Doctor just advised not to bother starting her up again on some of them, e.g. Nitrazepam or Lisinopril.

Back to the equipment. First due to the arthritis in her knees we installed a stair lift which has been invaluable. It took Jemima a while to get used to it and in the early stages would still try to walk up the stairs. In her latter stages it is more difficult to get her into the chair and once in it to ensure she doesn't try to climb out mid stair or trap her feet between the stair and the chair.

Next, after falling out of bed a couple of times both at home and in the hospital we now have a loaned hospital bed with sides and buttons to move the bed around in many different directions. All of which have benefited us over the years. Jemima, however, hates the sides and spends most of her time trying to escape, and believe me even with arthritis, she has managed to do just that. The first time was 3am one morning when I found not only had she climbed over the side but had managed to manoeuvre herself on top of a chest of drawers and there we found her, stark naked with a towel wrapped round her, swinging her legs and singing. She has managed to escape several times since but how she does it we have no idea and of course Jemima can't remember!

The bath lift has been a real boon, however, more difficult to use now that Jemima has a strong will to decide midway that she wants out of it. I am going to attempt it when D'Artagnan is around as I just know that if it is just me she is bound to act up.

A syringe is perfect for getting medicine into Jemima, or even drinks when she is in her more comatose state. Fight with your doctor for medication in liquid form and if not then mashing bananas and mixing the pills is a good idea, although only add the medicine by the spoonful as Jemima often gets half way through and then starts spitting it out.

The commode has also been a great help as we keep it in her bedroom and that means not so far to go, especially when her legs are playing up. A couple of things puzzle me, why are these not sturdier as unless Jemima has both hands on the sides it has a tendency to tip. We got this from the hospital, free of charge, when she was last there. When I asked them about returning it they refused point blank saying that they don't have the facility to take back used equipment. This means every item of equipment loaned/given out, including crutches, etc has to be replaced by the hospital to ensure every patient has what they need when they leave. Surely it would be more cost effective to set up a small room somewhere where a couple of 'retired' people could service, disinfect and put the item back into circulation. It's no wonder our hospitals are short of money. In the interests of health and safety we have now purchased a sturdier commode which has wheels, enabling us to move Jemima around the bedroom and to the stair lift.

Likewise I have been given multiples of bandages, ointments and first aid packs by the hospital and community nurses that although not opened or needed yet, they refuse to take back!

The Community Occupational Therapist has come up with a perch stool, and believe me this is an invaluable piece of equipment. I leave it in the bathroom and Jemima perches on it while she washes. This means I can run around making her bed and sorting out her clothes while she happily and safely takes control of her washing.

Every day is a challenge for both Jemima and us and all the information, manuals and advice available cannot prepare you. Every person with the disease is different, every carer has their limitations, every member of the family will deal with this in their own way.

There are agencies available that you can pay to get sitters in, but I must admit we only used friends as carers. This is really because our initial experiences of agency staff has not been good. Having tried it twice, one stole money and one spent her time reading the newspaper rather than entertaining Jemima, it was essential for us to consider other alternatives. We have been very lucky to have 3 wonderful 'carers' who came and sat with Jemima for 3 hours each day when I was at work and had lunch with her and just chatted. Of course we did pay them the going rate and they were worth every penny. Unfortunately they were all in their 70s and Jemima's condition has meant she is now too difficult to handle, so we have had to let them go.

Well, we are in to 8 weeks of the wonder drug Memantine when it has suddenly stopped being so effective. Jemima's anxiety over her lack of memories has returned, without the full on aggressiveness, but now with her being adamant that the things we talk about, such as seeing her son over breakfast just didn't happen! I have found that saying "Oh yes it did" doesn't work. So she continues throughout the day feeling alternately belligerent, confused, anxious, sad and frustrated about her lack of ability to walk as well as she used to. I have re-instated the dose of the Bio-Melatonin which again seems to have improved her moods and keeps her somewhat subdued but at least not comatose. Still early days!

The arthritis in her knees has deteriorated rapidly on a daily basis. The pills from Italy are not so effective, or the creams that I rub on regularly. It is so hard to see the pain she suffers and not be able to make it better for her. The cortisone injections are ineffective now and she absolutely hates her daily outings in the wheelchair. I get over that quite easily by allowing her to walk from the house to the car or from the car to the supermarket when she then is grateful for the help of the wheelchair. It is evident that if we want her to remain living with us I shall have to fund some sort of transport chair for moving her between bed and the bathroom, or between her chair in the front room to the dining table.

Looking at Respite

D'Artagnan and I have decided to place Jemima in a respite home for just a week so we can get some 'us' time and try to bring back some of the closeness we both feel we have been losing. Just being able to sleep in the same bed, go out walking, ride our bikes, go out in the evening, all sound heaven. For me, uninterrupted sex, when and where we like will be the icing on the cake! Sleeping apart has definitely been the major drawback, as I see it, to keeping my sanity. I definitely feel I am struggling more with the whole "What am I doing with my life" question that surfaces whenever I have had a bad or difficult day with Jemima.

On the subject of respite we were absolutely amazed that having found a suitable place that the cost was an exorbitant £1300 for a week! Makes my 2.40 per hour look even worse. Of course there are cheaper places, but most of these seem to be in old Victorian houses which have stairs, twists and turns and far worse, they smell. The one we have chosen is purpose built and part of the same care group where Jemima attends her weekly Dementia club. The reviews for this home had been bad some 2 years previously which according to the ladies we saw, had been addressed and were no longer an issue. So what better than a home that has already been inspected and brought up to scratch. I suppose my big fear is that Jemima will love it and not want to return home with us. She struggles to know who we are from one minute to the next and just maybe being in a place where she doesn't see anything familiar will give her more peace of mind. We shall see what happens.

D'Artagnan and I have decided to stay at home rather than go on 'holiday', as having the house to ourselves seems just too good to miss! Although I have made sure that I expect to treat the time as a holiday and go out for breakfast, long walks, bike rides etc...

For us respite was the welcome break we both needed, although we didn't do anything we intended to do and the weather was bad. I missed Jemima and called every morning to see how she had fared. We didn't visit her, on the advice of the home, as they said it was more likely to upset her. I wish I had ignored their advice. Instead of filling the time constructively I found myself sitting around at the times I would normally be running around after her and felt I had lost the purpose of my current existence.

For Jemima, well she fared less well and the aftermath has been difficult for all of us. She felt abandoned and very unhappy, feeling frightened all the time without the constant reassurance she is used to. In fact I barely recognised the usually well kempt lady I was used to seeing each day. Her dress was haphazard and she looked so frail and old. I know this was probably due to the fact that I was used to seeing her everyday and a week away was a shock. However, her demeanor had returned to the days when she had been on strong drugs, so it was evident that they were keeping her subdued with something. Certainly not the drugs I left with them.

The first thing she said to me was "I don't like sex!". This was re-iterated every day for a week once home. It is so difficult to know what triggered this, as just because it was not something she had said before, you never know whether this is just a symptom of the advanced dementia or whether something had happened to her during the week. Little bits she has said lead me to believe that although I had stipulated she was not to be dressed or undressed by a male carer, this was the likely cause. She would have fought the male and when they were too strong for her she gave in. No doubt in her mind that she had been raped!

I see no point in pursuing this with the Care Home as I don't think anything will be resolved, but it has given us much food for thought and we won't be putting Jemima through this experience again. Although we have both worked hard to make Jemima feel at home again, there is no doubt that the damage has been done. She continually asks me if I am going to sell her and her fears and anxieties are worse than they ever were. The other day when she attended her Dementia club she refused point blank to sit next to a man. She constantly tells me she doesn't want a man! I hope with love and care we can alleviate the very real fear she now has.

Life at home has changed quite dramatically now as Jemima fears going out of the house at all. She sleeps most of the day and keeps us up at night with her anxieties. This has made a great change to my life now as our daily trips out, which gave me a sense of freedom and control, have all but stopped. D'Artagnan and I take it in turns to escape when he is not working. I am still working on trying to get her confidence back but also have to be aware that at her age Jemima does not have the energy or interest she used to have.

Well it has been about 3 months since Jemima was in respite care and she appears at last to have gotten over her bad experience and seems to have forgiven men in general. Enough that she will now sit next to them, although is still wary, and continually says she doesn't want to have a baby? As I explained to her if she was able to have a baby at her age we would be millionaires! However, it has left her with an innate sense of anxiety, although nowadays this is more to do with D'Artagnan and I. She worries constantly if we leave the room or go out but in a sense this has improved her willingness to move around the house, sit in the garden (to keep us in view), which in turn has improved her health. Now that we have got her stable on her dementia medication I have re-introduced her pain medicine for her knees. This means she is more active and spends less time in bed. I have also noticed that some of her lost memories are returning, she is more alert and it is just so lovely to hear her laugh again.

Well so much for the return of my lovely Jemima, within days of writing this it is evident that the dementia medication is no longer effective. Her stubbornness and belligerence have returned in full force. Difficult as before but hopefully I am better able to cope with these changing moods. Once more getting Jemima to take her medication has become a battle of wills although these are her battles and I no longer worry about it or even try to argue with her. I find the best thing is just to let her get on with it and eventually I get her to do the things I need her to do. So lots of patience is the key. She has refused to go to bed tonight and has sent me to my bed. Needless to say this is not going to happen as Jemima cannot be left on her own. I find things to do while leaving her to her own devices and she is currently trying to escape through the front door. Unfortunately for her I thought ahead and locked the doors. It doesn't really matter how prepared you think you are for these changes in her moods there is no pattern to follow.

Back to the medication, I have stopped the pain medication as Jemima is suffering with itching all over her body during the night again. A couple of days should see whether it is the medicine causing this irritation. More difficult times ahead for us all I fear as her Alzheimers becomes more apparent.

After waking the next morning Jemima had been her old self, happy, eating and taking her medication without a fight. Maybe it was the pain medication which was now out of her system. A result! However, I was counting my chickens, after a good sleep she woke and was back to her vitriol other self.

Another night, at least with Jemima in her bed, where she has been chatting now to either herself or her imaginary friends from 2am and this has lasted nonstop to the morning. Once again conversations with her result in continued accusations of murder and mayhem and eventually to me being ordered out of her bedroom.

After a lot of patience I managed to wash and dress Jemima and get her to her dementia club. She may not have a good day but for my sanity she will just have to cope. I am beginning to fear picking her up again as I do wonder just how many more days I can take. Picking her up was an adventure as just as I was about to get her in the car she was distracted and decided that she was not going to get in. Following her up the road, to ensure she didn't fall over, one of the carers from the Club came out and held on to her while I got the car, and between us we managed to get her in. The drive home was one of screaming and lifting her feet up on to the dashboard and kicking the window! I just don't know where she gets her strength from. The one thing I have come to realise is that Jemima's dementia club is becoming more and more for my benefit than for hers. It does make me feel guilty leaving her there but I know this one day's respite is essential to my wellbeing.

Surprises of all surprises Jemima has once again come out of her mood and is almost back to her lovely self. Although still anxious and frightened at least we can go out again and this we have done although as it is winter now not as often as I would like. D'Artagnan and I continue to take alternate nights and take turns to Jemima sit if either of us need to go out. So the burden is not so great on either of us.

Out of the blue Jemima has decided not to eat or drink and after 5 days of getting only enough to keep a sparrow alive she continues to be as strong as ever, albeit losing weight. Not a bad thing as she is definitely lighter than she was, so much easier to lift.

Talking to the Doctor it is now evident that Jemima has made a decision not to prolong her life any longer than necessary. She no longer takes her medicine and most days refuses to dress. Her Doctor says we should just let her follow the natural course and not attempt to force food, drink or medication down her. Something we have never done although it is hard to continue standing aside knowing we are watching her move closer to dying. We try to keep her warm and happy, when she is willing. Both D'Artagnan and I have spent hours sitting by her bed, holding her hand, convinced that she is giving up, only to have her sit bolt upright in bed demanding food!

Today, she is alternating between calling me a stupid woman and singing songs at the top of her voice. Her arthritis is more painful with the lack of pain medicine.

It is now a month since we thought Jemima was giving up and today she is eating, sleeping (occasionally), and fit as a fiddle. Even the virus that is going round doesn't stop her. I have given up on the Doctor who continues his intransigence in prescribing Jemima's sleeping pills and the reduction to a half tablet just makes her dozy and therefore no sleep for either her or whichever one of us is on duty that night. We are once again trying some alternatives, such as the Bio-Melatonin and over the counter Nytol, but to no avail. We are going to try a her with a herbal option (Valerium) and see how she gets on with that next.

A couple of weeks on and nothing seems to work, however, she seems to have got herself in a pattern of staying awake for 2 or 3 days, catnapping at night and continuing to try and escape her bed, talking to imaginary people and singing in her sleep.

She will then spend a couple of days constantly asleep and will not leave her bed! I am slowly taking her off her sleeping pills as she misses so many doses due to the Doctor not fulfilling her prescription promptly. I am also considering putting her back on to her anti-depressants.

How about this, I recently bought a walker, 3 wheels, for Jemima, which was faulty when it arrived, so after calling them to complain they immediately sent me a new one, next day with free delivery. When asked if the driver would collect the faulty one, I was advised to keep it for spares. So all in all, having managed to mend the first one we now have two, one for upstairs and one for down. Now all I need to do is get Jemima away from her walking stick and using the new wheels! As a matter of interest, I took Jemima to one of those disabled stores for her to try out the 3 wheeler and even took it home to try there and given the option to return it if she didn't take to using it. I did return it as the cost was £90 and after finding it on the Internet I now have two for the cost of £35! Well worth shopping around. Don't get me wrong, Jemima deserves the best, but at her age I can see little point in spending the money unnecessarily, especially as the second hand prices for disabled equipment is so much lower, and in the back of my mind I hope for Jemima's sake that her suffering does not go on for much longer. When she does use the wheels you would be amazed at just how fast she moves on her own! Her memory function is the major drawback as she forgets how to use it from one moment to the next.

An interesting change in Jemima, although we had sorted out her medication, which she now seems settled with, she was so depressed, anxious, worried and crying. She had been on anti-depressants since her 80's when going through the problems with her husband, however, during our medication review I had taken her off these. After discussions with her doctor we decided to re-instate the anti-depressants. In fact the other day she said she felt so much more confident and less frightened and we would have many long conversations about the memories she still has, even though they are well and truly mixed up.

After 3 weeks the change in her mental health is so much better. She smiles when I wake her in the morning, laughs and sings all day, and loves a cuddle before she goes to sleep. She has taken to working during the night with her colleagues from the Royal Air Force (1942-1945) who she sees regularly in her bedroom. She organises and bosses them around to ensure all her duties are carried out. It appears that she keeps them in line and she will often be heard telling them off. D'Artagnan pops up at about 11pm and sends everyone home, only to find she has secreted one of the girls under her bed covers and as soon as he leaves the room she carries on working. I have learnt that once she is watered and fed and been to the toilet to just turning down the monitor so I only hear her when she yells for me. Unfortunately for D'Artagnan he hears every word!

Although this concerned us to begin with we both realise that this is good for Jemima as her vocabulary and social interaction is regular and during these hours her mental state and memory are almost normal. As she now sleeps most of the day we just let her get on with her nightly conversations, turn down her monitor, and get a good night sleep! Well some nights!

These latter stages of Dementia create more problems as her memory span gets shorter and shorter. She will ask for the toilet and once there, (if she doesn't change her mind on the way), will forget what she is there for and in some instances will fight me all the way. Better to just agree and try again later when perhaps she will be in a more conducive mood. Whatever happens the hardest part is maintaining the patience with her, as once upset, she will worry that she has upset me. Every day is an adventure, a mountain to climb, a frozen lake to slip on, or just deep into the water feet first. The most you can do is to keep your loved one safe and follow their lead.

Trying to keep Jemima at home is becoming more of a battle than we ever anticipated. The Doctor came round, after I had recently complained that he had rejected her anti-inflammatory prescription. Since taking this medicine I have managed to keep Jemima off the pain killers. Within 4 days of coming off the medicine Jemima was screaming in pain and is now bed bound. However, you could have knocked me down with a feather when he came round one evening, waving a piece of paper, just like the 'Peace in our Time' letter, telling me he was not prepared to continue providing the drugs I had 'ordered'. Excuse me, but you are the one who has been prescribing this for the last 18 months! Now he tells me he is not prepared to be sued or done for manslaughter if he continues prescribing. No amount of logic could get through to him. Surely a shorter good quality of life is better than a long bad quality of life in pain? Apparently not, and he went away threatening us with Social Services as we were trying to dope Jemima! No referral was made and a month later I telephoned the Adult Care department at our local council to try and get someone to come to help me with lifting and manage transferring Jemima around the house. I am not a nurse but even I can see that Jemima needs some sort of physiotherapy and I need training in how to lift her without damaging her. All looked good until I mentioned that due to the Doctor's recent withdrawal of Jemima's anti-inflammatory medicine she was now screaming with the pain whenever I tried to move her. Resulting sometimes in her just collapsing, almost comatose, while trying to manage her from her commode to her bed. Not so bad, but when it happens half way across the room, we have a problem. The Doctor's answer is that I should carry on applying the useless anti-inflammatory gel he prescribed, or call him when it gets too bad and he will admit her to hospital or administer a dose of morphine. Neither of which any of us want to happen. Anyway, back to my latest saga. The Adult Care cannot take the referral without the Doctor coming out to see her to do an Emergency Assessment. Then, and only then, will the Responsive Service take the referral, who then decide whether Jemima needs the help or not!

So now we have Proactive Services, Responsive Services and District Nurses all involved. We get visits almost every day while they try to sort out the next steps for Jemima. Ultimately they now class her as 'End of Life', and I have the dreaded injections in a cupboard as a constant reminder.

Jemima seems quite happy staying in bed and her dementia continues at a manageable level for both of us. The nurse this morning said I was to encourage Jemima to use the nappy pants, rather than get her out of bed. As I explained, Jemima will not do this, she values her dignity. She would rather not drink anything than take the chance of wetting her bed or herself. So against their wishes D'Artagnan and I continue to put her on her commode, although it definitely takes both of us now.

We now have visits once a week unless I call them to insert suppositories to keep on top of her constipation. This shouldn't go on too long as Jemima is not taking any medicines that contribute to the problem, and her eating and drinking has reduced considerably.

It is now almost a month since Jemima was at death's door and bedridden. For the last 2 weeks she has been delightful, full of cheer, singing and seems quite used to her new status and relieved that she does not have to come downstairs or go out. As she sleeps most of the day my time is now spent with her whenever she is awake, seeing to whatever she feels she needs. I have set up a routine of getting Jemima out of bed for meals and find that if we sing a song she will dance across the room with a smile on her face. Some days she falls asleep in the chair and others she asks to go back to bed. We spend most afternoons chatting, singing or just reminiscing dependent on her mood. She has days where she eats constantly and others when she refuses all but a few drops of water. Both D'Artagnan and I often sit beside her bed as her breathing becomes shallow and we both think that she will go any minute, but so far her little heart just fights on.

This morning she woke up and the first thing she said to me was "Kill me"! It breaks my heart as it is evident that she has had enough of being the way she is. Dementia is such a strange disease, how can she not remember how to do the simplest thing or recognise very much at all, and yet can be so aware of her condition.

There have been many times over the last few years when I wished I could go back and make a different choice, walk away from the responsibility, and go back to having a life. However, Jemima's fighting spirit, her lovely smile and those songs in the middle of the night make me realise why I do this and will no doubt continue until her last breath is taken. Hopefully at home with her family rather than in some Hospital or Care Home.

All of this brings me back to the concept of my book, the choices we make and the consequences of those decisions. Never in my wildest dreams was I really prepared for what looking after Jemima meant. 16 years so far, sharing my home with another woman, 12 of these years getting to grips with dementia, each year being more difficult and restricting than the one before. The effect it has had on my relationship with the rest of the family and my marriage. If I hear one more person tell me what an angel I am and how I will get my reward in heaven, I have no doubt that I might just hurry that reward up! We all like to be appreciated but ultimately I think everyone would prefer the help rather than the platitudes.

For those of you who do not have the help I have with D'Artagnan, do get in touch with the Carer Associations and find out how you can get the respite you need. Whether this is just getting someone to sit with your loved one for an afternoon a week or finding a dementia club, as I have, where you can get time out without the worry. There is no doubt in my mind that if you try to look after a loved one on your own, you will in the end destroy your own self-worth and in all likelihood come to blame the very person you are trying so hard to care for, for this loss of independence.

BEING A CARER

Although I have touched on the work involved in being a personal carer I thought maybe it would be better to share my days with you.

A typical day – well there just isn't one! No day is the same as any other. Each morning, irrespective of how the night has gone, is a surprise just waiting to happen.

Anyway let me just lay out the duties involved in looking after someone of 96 with dementia and arthritis.

My morning starts with taking Jemima to the toilet and then either back to bed, depending on the time, or downstairs for breakfast and then back to bed for a while. I say a while, as this can be 5 minutes or 3 hours depending on her.

Next, to the bathroom for a wash and then dress for the day, followed by brunch. Eating little and often is how Jemima copes with eating as she finds it a tedious effort. I have started to feed her at her request, and at least this way I can get more than a couple of spoonful's into her. She loves her food and is happy to break the day up with these events.

Washing up and clearing the house is carried out while Jemima sits in her chair downstairs and has a nap. She will often help with the drying up of the dishes, although her knees make this more difficult for her so she now sits at the table and I hand her the items one at a time. However, this small contribution to the housework is very satisfying for Jemima and makes her feel better and not so reliant on me. It is important to keep her entertained or focussed throughout her waking moments so she has little time to give in to her anxieties.

Lunch and then possibly out shopping, although this again is dependent on Jemima's mood of the day. I can assure you that you should not attempt outings when the dementia sufferer is feeling aggressive or out of sorts. Again these outings are good for Jemima to be able to be part of daily life, meeting new people and getting her to cope with different situations. Otherwise I spend most of the afternoon sitting holding her hand and chatting or singing with her. This is interspersed with afternoon tea as Jemima just loves cakes!

Late afternoon I include Jemima in the preparation of dinner, which isn't as easy as it sounds as Jemima cannot use implements or in fact remember how to peel a potato, let alone what a potato is some days. She sets the table and when she isn't looking I put everything in the right place.

We all sit down together at the table for our meal. Although some nights Jemima doesn't feel like eating it is good to keep routines going. A bowl of ice cream always works!

A half hour letting our meal go down and again chatting with Jemima as the television is not an option. I have tried with different programmes but it doesn't really matter what it is as she then gets anxious about all these people in the house.

Wash and bed time which can take anything from 30 minutes to an hour depending on whether I have to persuade her of the efficacy of a good night's sleep and to remove her clothes of course. Then it is prayers and chat to allay her fears once again that it is alright to fall asleep and that she is Home and Safe. These words are our mantra and seem to work.

Then the evening is mine? No such luck, we keep an eye on the baby monitor and spend most evenings responding to Jemima, either to reassure her, feed her, or convince her that it is too early to get out of bed.

The night is mine? Well sort of. D'Artagnan and I take it in turns to sleep in the office so that whoever is on duty can respond and deal with Jemima while at least one of us gets some sleep. When on duty overnight

I can sometimes get a couple of hours unbroken sleep, but that is the unusual rather than the norm.

Next morning we start all over again and who knows what the day will bring. We manage a bath once a week, again depending on her mood, but she tolerates me doing her hair now. She always used to go to the hairdresser, but nowadays she finds this a real strain unless I sit with her for the 2 hours or so when she has a perm. So now I wash, cut and set her hair at least once a week.

As Jemima's condition deteriorates so does my day. As she now remains in bed, except for popping on the commode, both D'Artagnan and I have more time together. I have more time in the home as she sleeps almost constantly, waking only for meals or toilet. I just can't believe how tidy and clean my house is now!

For me, as the prime carer, I have approached my life with Jemima as a job of work. When I retired and took to looking after Jemima full time I realised quite early on that the only way I could deal with the emotions of looking after a close relative was to treat it as a full-time job. Tackling the day to day care with planning and preparation with Jemima's wellbeing at the centre of it all. Of course nothing can prepare you for the full-time aspect of being a carer as 24/7 means just that! The carer/attendance allowance supplements my pension and enables us to maintain our standard of living, although I do wonder at the Government assuming that without a pension the allowance itself works out at just under 2.40p per hour! I wonder what happened to the minimum living wage? Evidently only for carers who spend 15 minutes a day with a patient.

I appreciate every hour I get off and try to make the most of the time. The one thing I can say is that I have always taken on different jobs that present a challenge and as you may have read in my work chapter, I did tend to leave when the challenge was no longer there. Every day is a challenge, not only in just getting Jemima through the day, but also maintaining my own sanity and needs. This is where you need to ensure that you get some respite.

I try to get my hair done every month as it is just so easy to become a slob at home not worrying too much how I look and sometimes not even brushing my hair all day. I go and sit in the sun or a café when the weather is bad and write my book or just sit and people watch. In the summer I go up the park and walk and exercise on the gym equipment dotted around. Costs nothing and last year it really helped me tone up and keep fit. Walking at a snail's pace most days really doesn't help, so my advice is to get away from the house and the person you are caring for whenever time allows.

I have a different outlook on housework, no longer able to give it the usual weekly clean throughout as I used to do when I was working full time, now I fit it in around Jemima. The hardest thing I found about this is that housework is just never ending, I can never sit down and say 'Well that's it done for another week"! Accept the changes to your life and embrace them as just part of your new job. In fact for someone who hates housework this works so much better for me as I no longer stress about the house and as long as I keep it tidy and fit in hoovering, dusting etc each day. So not necessarily hoovering the whole house as just one room at a time. Washing and ironing last all week but I can do the dreaded ironing a bit at a time over the week.

Well that is the physical part of being a carer now for the mentality needed to take on looking after anyone of this age, irrespective of the health aspects.

When I started I was already on anti-depressants, please do read my chapter on workplace bullying, as this will give you the background as to why I am on them.

Over the past 3 years my Doctor has tried to get me to come off these pills or at least reduce them and this year I tried for 2 months, first reducing the dosage on odd days and then eventually taking the reduced dosage every day. Within a week I was changing from the patient, happy carer I was into a depressed slob, resenting my life, and crying at the drop of a hat. I only did this for 2 weeks before I decided to go back on my full dosage. The one thing you cannot do when you are a carer is to have health problems yourself, although Jemima says she will look after me if I do get ill! Sweet!

I feel I am in a catch 22 situation, damned if I do and damned if I don't. So many of the friends and family tell me that Jemima is still alive because of the great care I give her. I almost feel to blame that she is still suffering and eventually had a discussion with D'Artagnan about what I should do. Do I stop giving her sustenance as they do with the hospital and care home pathways where they deliberately let people die, or do I carry on knowing that every drop of water or food I give her is just delaying the inevitable. Especially when it is evident Jemima just wants to die.

Not a decision I can make or even bring myself to carry out, but D'Artagnan has convinced me that when Jemima goes it must be naturally and not forced by my actions, and although I agree, I find it so hard to just ignore her heartfelt pleas to end it all.

I suppose for me the hardest thing is the hurtful things she says to me. I know she doesn't mean it but how can someone who has spent her whole life being a lovely person turn into being vindictive, mean and nasty. I try hard to ignore it but found myself in tears today as she continued to tell me what a terrible person I am and how my Mother must be so ashamed of having a daughter like me. Last night she accused me of murdering her brother during the war and of course reasoning with her that I wasn't even born when her brother died means absolutely nothing to her.

For Jemima it must be so difficult to be in such a state of confusion and no doubt she must have someone that she can vent her anger on. As I am the one closest and most frequently with her it is not surprising really.

Unfortunately this is not a job I can walk away from, but I do know that the challenge will never end. I am very sure, however, that like the time I built the patio in the back garden, I will only ever do this once!

GOING FORWARD

Well after many redrafts and edits I think I have achieved what I set out to do in writing this book. Much of it was for my benefit and has proved as cathartic as I hoped it would be. There are of course lots in life still on-going with, in some cases, no hope of a resolution and those that will be resolved in the fullness of time.

I always remember what my Mother said to me a month before she died and I try hard to live with her doctrine on life.

"Life is but a series of adventures taking us through the different ages of growth, some are good and some are bad. Live life to the full and appreciate the good, learn from the bad, and put those experiences down to lessons learnt."

Remember you can share your experiences, giving help and advice when asked, but everyone is different and each person needs to deal with their own, finding the way that works for them. Some are braver than others and able to sort themselves out and some need to seek the help they need. Ultimately though it is down to us as individuals to live this relatively short life to the full and you shouldn't make anyone do what they don't want to do.

Overall I have made many mistakes through my life which have inadvertently affected so many around me. Some I learnt from, some I have only just realised, and in writing this book I have learnt so much about myself.

The choices I have made are mine, with no one else to blame for the consequences of those choices, but overall I have been luckier than most and look forward to my next adventure in life.

----------------------The Adventure Starts Here----------------------

The New Year started with Petie our cat having to be put down as he became very ill. Fortunately, he was no longer able to make the stairs and by the time we had to take the decision, Jemima had forgotten all about him. With Jemima now 97 years old we have decided not to replace Petie so as not to tie ourselves down in the future.

I have decided to wean myself off my anti-depressants and so far things are going well. If I am to start this new adventure then I need to be in control and this is the start of it.

Out of the blue we received a telephone call from our Grandson asking if he could come and see us, bringing D'Artagnan's daughter, my Stepdaughter, and arranged a time that suited them. Unfortunately they didn't bother turning up. No call to say why or to re-arrange, so once again we have come to the conclusion that there is little hope of rectifying the situation or of meeting our new great-grandson.

Oh Oh! Just found several lumps in one of my breasts, looks like my next adventure is unlikely to be what I wanted or expected. Now there will probably only be one choice and a question of who will go first, me or Jemima!

Lightning Source UK Ltd.
Milton Keynes UK
UKHW040329120119
335448UK00001B/34/P